PLANET EROPMANOP

PLANET EROPMANOP

PLANET

EROPMANOP

A NOVEL

LOU BALDIN

PLANET EROPMANOP

ISBN: 9781521327883

A SLICE OF LIFE IN OUR COSMIC CORNER

Contents

Ego-driven souls, we are not; we simply possess immense latitude of freedoms that are unknown and out of reach to the physically-endowed life forms (humans) that make up a large percentage of the biological mass of the universe.

PROLOGUE

To the readers of this book, be forewarned that the insane story written on the pages of this book comes from the twisted and warped imagination of the author. For those inclined to continue reading after this warning be sure to thank your god, your lucky stars, or the tooth fairy that the material that follows is only FICTION! Or, is it?

TAKEN

My house shook so hard that I thought it was going to explode off the stone foundation. A fierce thunderstorm had whipped up out of nowhere that evening and pounded the house with phenomenal amounts of rain and golf ball size hail that left my green lawn covered with mounds of ice from the barrage. It was a warm July evening and only moments had passed after the sun had set that the storm hit. Flashes of lightning lit up the darkened sky and gave me glimpses of the shadowy and menacing monster-storm and clouds that created the near hurricane-like winds. The fierce winds blew the trees in my front yard nearly sideways and sheared leaves and small shoots off the tree branches and scattered them over my lawn and driveway.

Next thing I know, I'm viewing my house from up high above the treetops and from inside of the dark stormy clouds. My mind was awash with fear that overwhelmed me as adrenaline raced to every nerve in my body and panic began to mount in my mind. I thought that I must have been sucked up by a tornado that had barreled down and gobbled up my house and me along with it. Moments passed, and I'm still standing upright, unfrazzled and unscathed and extremely calm, but confused about what was holding me up in the air over my house. I then find

20

myself inside of a strange vehicle, a ship and looking through a porthole, and peering down at my house below, which was completely intact and firmly sitting on the rock foundation, with no apparent damage that I could tell from my bird's eye view.

I'm in the clouds inside of a strange and blindingly bright ship straight out of a science fiction horror movie and stunned like a deer in the headlights of an oncoming car. The storm and my house are now the last things on my mind as I grapple with and try and make sense of what just happened to me. The thought in my head, grabbing all the attention was, "where the hell am I."

Profoundly lost in my whole thought processes, I nearly passed out from the sheer shock and mental whiplash created by the drama whirling around in my thoroughly confused mind. Moments of calm and then anxiety took turns at the helm of my whole being. The ordeal triggered rapid mood swings as I have never experienced in my life before, not even as a soldier in a combat situation, as I have been during my military days.

Like most people on Earth, I was aware of the UFO phenomenon and had heard the crazy, outlandish, and bizarre claims from UFO theorists and the UFO nut crowd that storm clouds sometimes shielded (hid) within them Alien craft, flying saucers, UFOs or top secret military vehicles mistaken as UFOs. But I was never interested or motivated in looking into the phenomena or doing any research on UFOs because it seemed a silly subject to engage. One of the farmers who lives nearby my house and that I did some work for told me he had seen strange lights in the sky one night, and asked me if I had seen the lights. I didn't and didn't pursue that UFO topic of conversation from utter lack of interest. Now, I wished I had paid more attention about Alien beings from space.

I wasn't over the shock from the storm that rattled my house and my nerves to the bone, which left me shaken and in panic mode. And now I had to deal with the fact that I was inside of a god-damned UFO, up, up in the clouds over my house. I was almost pissed off about the ordeal that my mind was put through, and was desperate to make sense of my unfolding bizarre situation.

In my oddly gyrating and now calm state, I stood at the window of the UFO watching the storm that continued battering my poor house down below. I should've been shook-up and petrified rather than calm and serene, but I had become suddenly bipolar with my erratic emotions. I wasn't sure if my transient tranquility on the heels of my adrenalin rush caused by the storm was due to the adrenaline receding out of my system or if it was a separate altogether psychotic reaction of my mind collapsing from simultaneous mind-altering events. The

UFO and my apparent Alien abduction hadn't completely sunk in yet, but it was certainly gnawing on the door of my fragile, exhausted and confounded mind.

I lived in the Midwest, where horrific thunder and lightning storms along with the risk of tornadoes were a common and constant concern during the spring and early summer season. However, throughout all the horrific storms I've been through, I had never seen or experienced a tornado my whole life. That night in that wicked storm, I fully expected that a tornado was about to rip my house and me to shreds and scatter the debris over countless acres of farmer's fields from where my house stood.

My mind shifted back to the ship that I found myself inside of and that now held me, prisoner. My mind raced back and forth from the storm predicament to how did I get inside this alien flying machine? And where are my captors, the Aliens that abruptly and clearly abducted me? I wondered to myself, but in no way, did I want them to show themselves if they looked like and were anything like the Hollywood variety that I had seen at the movie theaters. I was bewildered but nonetheless, felt safe inside this strange hovering contraption veiled by the menacing storm clouds.

I was inside of a mysterious Alien ship that presumably, possibly, saved me from a thunderstorm? Had it been a tornado that Aliens saved me from, that would make sense. I could then tell my friends and family, "I was saved by the gods, or by my guardian angels from a tornado that leveled my house. And by the way, guardian angels and or gods, have spaceships." I'm sure that would go over well.

The more I thought about my irrational situation inside the UFO, the more I cringed. Nevertheless, where was the sheer panic that was missing? My mind-speak was trying to do just that, create panic in my mind with images of strange alien creatures come to Earth to suck my brains out and leave my brainless carcass a bumbling zombie mess.

The freaky alien image was going berserk in the back of my mind as I cautiously walked around the circular craft not sure if I should instead be running and in a panic of sorts. However, outright terror, the number one thing in these sort of situations, from the little I have read, was missing, and so was my adrenalin, which should have been off the charts as it was during the thunderstorm. Something about the ship's interior was soothing, intoxicating, relaxing, and kept me in a state of calmness. Perhaps it was the ship's subtle way of luring me like an insect into a deadly embrace of an Alien version of a carnivorous Venus flytrap.

I continued walking with ever increasing curiosity, and fewer episodes of anxiety as my acceptance of the bizarre alien ship incrementally grew on me. Portholes appeared every so often as I made my way around the perimeter of the ship and then they disappeared, blinked out of sight when I passed by the highly mysterious windows. I could see the lightning flashes boiling over inside of the clouds from the portholes, with a view that is so much clearer than when I was inside my house and looking out the window up at the storm. I did not hear the loud thunderclaps as I did when I was inside my house, which shook the house as if lightning had hit the house or one of the nearby trees.

In sharp contrast to the way that the rain struck the windows of my house like a battering ram hammering against the windows, I heard no sounds in the ship up to that point. The ship didn't rock back and forth like a boat on stormy seas lost in the waves washing over it. The ship was unaffected by the storm's unyielding thrashing even as sheets of rain pelted it and the tenacious wind and rapid-fire bursts of lightning enveloped the ship in a cocoon of water and an electrified mesh made from the furious sparks of plasma.

The interior of the ship was strange and seemed to lack a solidified hard surface. It was like walking on cushy and colorful pavement in a strange land or a children's

25

playground at a park, rather than inside of a super advanced Alien spaceship. The feel was fresh and liberating, a feeling I would imagine if I were walking in a field of blooming and fragrance-rich flowers on a warm and slightly breezy sunny afternoon. There was no breeze or movement of air inside the ship, but the mysterious movement of something that remained hidden and elusive inside of the ship, shivered my spine from the moment that I found myself on the UFO. I ambled around the colorful corridor unhurried, and frequently, more times than I can remember; and at times, appeared to have made little headway or progress as if I was walking in a loop where time stood still or time disappeared altogether.

Untroubled by my lack of progression through the ship, I managed to thoroughly enjoy my causal wondering and the embellished vistas that each passing moment ushered to me as if invisible beings showered me with gentle, subtle gifts for my senses; when in fact, I should have been scared out of my senses.

The inside of the ship was a winding circular corridor like a spiral of a seashell but lacking a definitive incline or the feel of a downward or upward motion as I occasionally hurried as if being pushed while I made my way around it and through the spiral. I wasn't walking or running in circles (I didn't think) but moving forward inside of a circular passageway that was a mass of contradictions to my human perceptions and overly excited and battered senses. Each step I took and made placed me deeper in the enticing innards, the guts, of the marvelous and wonderfully spooky Alien ship.

The ship's bowels blazed and oozed various shades of colors of unimaginable brilliance that pricked like thundering hail at my nearly obliterated mind, body, and soul. Colors of multifaceted rainbows adorned with hues and pastels and so much more that I strain to describe the symphony of textures that overwhelmed me. Colors that I had never been aware of before while on Earth that perhaps I failed to notice because the colors on earth didn't jump out at me and hit me in the gut, and grab me by the throat and then slap me around to seize my full, undivided attention.

The frequencies and hues that dazzled were a form of silent communications like road signs that suggested that I had traveled to new panoramas within the ship and to prove that time had not stopped or, at least, that I was in motion and moving towards something. Like on a walking trail through a forest offers new vistas of trees and plants with differing landscapes, serving as markers, so that one can differentiate segments of the trail and judge progression through the forest.

I knew not how long I strolled or how long I was on the alien ship. Time itself seemed absent and an absolute illusion, which accounted for my blissful and contradicting confusion. If time existed on the ship, it might have morphed into something far more mysterious than what my mere human senses grasped about the paradox of what time is. My watch had stopped working and remained frozen on the exact moment of time I entered the ship. Therefore, time, as I understood it, had stopped and become null and void to my normal way of thinking of what time is or was. That was an indication or confirmation that "something else" was in the mix of my new emerging reality.

That sense of a different flow of reality, that kept me from bunching up and running into myself, as if in some bizarre, warped dimension. Intrigued I was, but not as much as if such a thing had happened to me on Earth. I felt more energized than I had ever felt in my entire life and wasn't sure if I could attribute that to the skewed time factor or something else in the Alien ship. Nevertheless, my primary focus was now on my newfound vigor that had no physical or mental bounds!

The raw dynamism that radiated out of my pores like electrified sparks flitting off plasma, filled me with wild expectations of what was to come inside the amazing ship. I was in my thirties and had plenty of energy and vigor, but nothing like the surge that enraptured and enveloped my whole being soon after my capture by the Alien ship. My mind and body profoundly merged while going through enormous, yet subtle, changes during my casual stroll down, in, and around mystery lane.

Continuously, from the serene, colorful and vibrant reality, emerged vistas brand new, which added more flavors to titillate the already gorged senses of body and mind. My walk, stride, and glide, around the ship's colorful passageway, gave way and merged with abstract symbols and confusing patterns embedded into the curved walls, yet, in my face; and swathed with geometric and scrambled holographic motifs of living breathing monsters, hiding in the cracks and crevices of the ship.

The parade of strangeness floated and bobbed as if on ocean waves and currents and visible radio waves silently engulfed the air and space that escorted me to God-knows-where. They were things, designs and weird shapes that made no sense but added pleasurable aspects to my ever increasing and expanding experiences as I traveled placidly and wantonly down the tube-like channel of a hallway.

I continued in my awkward gait in the Alien version of Alice in Wonderland, the uncanny and positively peculiar it became, the deeper into the odd places of cosmic foreplay I slid forever into. I perceived a change inside of my aura when my skin glowed and sparked, covered in colorful electrical waves of plasma that left my whole body no longer in the dark. Auras on the ship are far more mysterious than the little I've heard about them in the past back on Earth. Up until now, I was entirely unsure that such biological magic existed, and wouldn't have believed it existed without seeing it for myself. I had heard and seen a demonstration on a television show that I once watched, briefly, that all living things, plants, and animals exude auras and now I know that to be true. My whole body glowed a colorful perplexing ambient array of aura and a flashlight in the dark spaces on the ship my body became.

While spiraling along in mind, body and soul, I noticed, from looking out of the opulent and ever-present and palpitating porthole, that the ship was no longer inside of the storm clouds. The ship wasn't perched over my house, as it had been only moments earlier, but was now traveling at a frenzied and fantastically dizzying speed towards some unknown "object", somewhere in deep space. I knew not what that "object" was that the ship scrambled with all its might to reach, I only knew, somehow, that the ship was heading towards a mysteriously large object with apparent and fervent urgency.

That should have concerned me, being that I was whisked away, taken far from my family, my home, my planet and the only life of my awareness from the first day of my birth. I was not the least bit concerned or worried or traumatized by my abduction and about the fact that my past, and everything about who or what I was, was vanishing before my eyes. Instead, I peered out the large eye-shaped porthole, which kept changing shape, and enthusiastically and symbolically waved goodbye and good riddance to planet Earth and my now former human life and existence.

On Earth, I lived alone, and the life of a fool, clouded in mind and body in my absurd Darwinian beliefs that humans are the progeny of scum that originated by accident in some ancient primordial cesspool. And furthermore, could most probably be, per the leading scientific minds, the only intelligent life form that came out of the abyss of nothingness in the whole of the universe and us humans were most likely all there was. It is excruciatingly and abundantly clear to me now that such notions are blatantly false and patently idiotic.

I lived some distance from a major metropolitan city out in what people refer to as the sticks, boonies or boondocks. Surrounding my property are miles of dense timberland but also cattle ranches, bean fields and boundless acres of corn fields—parcels of farmland that interrupted the continuity of the forestland. The country air was sweet and unpolluted, and the sounds of nature are soothing to my restless soul.

I fell in love with that country feeling when out for a drive one day and noticed a for-sale sign on the house that I now own. The house had sat vacant and on the market for two years, and I was able to buy the house at a price that I could not walk away from. I negotiated an owner finance with ten percent down, signed the contract and locked it up that same day. I moved into my house two weeks later.

I loved the seclusion and tranquility away from the city lights, and away from the noise and the trash-talk of urban living. Country life, far away from the burgeoning crowds, afforded me a serenity that was unknown to me while I was growing up in a large metropolitan area and densely populated inner-city neighborhood next to a part of town that is now bludgeoned, decimated, and bloodied by gangs and gang graffiti.

My house in the sticks was less than an hour away from a major city and only a few minutes from a small suburban bedroom community, where I did my shopping and congregating a few times a week for groceries and light entertainment, when I took in a movie at the only cinema they had in town. I socialized in the town with a few army buddies at the local VFW (veterans of foreign wars) and occasionally involved myself with the functions the VFW provided. I was not a regular at the VFW as most of the members were, and sometimes weeks, if not months, passed between my participation in the activities and meetings. Working for a living to pay the bills consumed much of my time.

I was single and dated off and on some of the girls living in the small town. Nothing ever cemented between any of them and me, which made me wonder if something was wrong with me. I'm not a stud, but I am a little above average in the looks department and had no shortage of dates with women.

I served in the Army four years, saw a little combat action in a war zone in the Middle East, not much, but it was enough to start me taking life a bit more seriously than I had up to that point. A borderline care-free lifestyle was my aim, and I had made some progress in achieving that means of living, stashing away funds rather than frittering my money on mindless activities at the bar and pool hall. I witnessed things in that war that woke me from my sheltered life as an over-indulged American boy growing up in a well-to-do family, from an upper-middle-class atmosphere in a well-kept and meticulously manicured part of town. However, by the time I finished my military contract and returned to civilian life, my old hood had lost some of its luster, when surrounding neighborhoods deteriorated, and property values tanked.

I joined the army for the promise to see the world and see it, I did. The ravaged and horrific underbelly of human despair, that prevailed in the places the army deployed me. Countries and people's lives tormented by endless wars, did a lot to make me realize and appreciate the comforts and the true miracles that peace, freedom, and prosperity provided to those people that cherished them. The things my generation and I, and generations before, have taken for granted and, for some, have lost.

In the army, I specialized in intelligence gathering and was not so much involved in the fighting. I was not an officer but could have been, had I followed in my father's footsteps, and taken his advice and joined the academy of his alma mater. I had no desire for a lengthy military career as an officer and settled for joining as an enlisted man instead. I did become a non-commissioned officer (NCO), a sergeant during my abbreviated military career.

Four years in the army matured me considerably, and for that, I was grateful for the opportunity to serve my country; not to mention the generous benefits the Army provided me after my honorable discharge. I used some of that education money to learn a trade suitable for re-engaging back into civilian life. I considered going to college on the GI bill, but I didn't want to spend four years in school.

As a civilian, I earned my living doing construction work in the town near where I lived. I was handy with a hammer and loved working outdoors; making repairs and building new decks and other types of projects. I learned my carpentry skills at a trade school in the city, and the practical hands-on, trial and error, while doing small jobs here and there around town, wherever I could find work. I started out doing small jobs with people I knew in town and odds and ends for some of the farmers near where I lived. I'm a jack-of-all-trades and master of none, as the saying goes, but I did master a few things, enough to keep me busy and people calling me back with additional construction projects they wanted me to do for them. I never worked for a company and was self-employed my entire life, which I consider a blessing, even though the paychecks were not steady or reliable.

I flipped houses when the remodeling jobs slowed down. I purchased homes in need of repairs and fixed them up, then sold them or rented them if I couldn't sell them quick enough, which made me a landlord for a time. I reluctantly gave rentals a try but being a landlord was not my forte, my style, I soon learned the hard way. I didn't possess the mandatory skills of a landlord, the brutal temperament required to survive in the rental business. When my renters didn't make their rent payments and gave me the sob story instead, I often buckled and let them off the hook and gave them more time (more time to come up with more excuses). That ended up costing me my good credit when I, in turn, was unable to make payments on the rental property to the bank. I tried everything in my power to make it work, but I ended up walking away from two of my rentals and let them go back to the lender. That destroyed my credit rating and my willingness to ever engage in the brutally unpredictable rental home business.

I was as busy as I wanted to be with my construction jobs and sometimes did just enough to get by (enough to pay the bills). I grew some of my vegetables on my five acres of land that my house sat on. Most of my land was in trees. One day, when I had nothing better to do, I cleared out a patch of trees and brush and turned a portion of my land into a vegetable garden and planted tomatoes, squash, green peppers, cucumbers, and my favorite, sweet corn. I planned on having fresh eggs and constructed a chicken coop and bought a few chickens. Somehow, a fox, raccoon, or some other critter, got in the hastily-built chicken house and ate my chickens. I gave up on that idea and bought my fresh eggs from a farmer not far from my house.

I heated my house during the winter months mostly with the dead wood I collected from fallen trees, cut them up with my chainsaw and split them with a log-splitter that I had acquired through a barter exchange for a job I did for a neighbor farmer friend. I had a pile of firewood stacked high up against the side of my barn with enough logs to last me through the winter months. Burning firewood put a substantial dent in my propane gas bills and gave me something cozy to look at while warming up my home on dreary cold days.

I hunted some of my food, turkeys, and deer when they were in season and sometimes when they weren't but happened onto my property. I froze the meat so that it lasted me through the year and that dropped my food expenses significantly. Fishing in a nearby lake provided me with fish to eat and an enjoyable and free venue for entertainment. Enthusiasm for most sports I didn't have and applied that energy to the challenge and the fight put up by the fish in their futile attempts to avoid my dinner plate.

The life I chose to live was not a lifestyle suited for most city folks and was probably one of the reasons I remained unhitched. I cherished my independence with a vengeance, and would never have settled for anything less, and that too figured into why I hadn't pursued the marriage route with any passion. However, I had a deep-down and veiled desire of, someday, finding a wife and raising a family. Now that I'm on some Alien spaceship and being whisked away to some other planet, I'm not sure what I'm in for in the marriage and family scenario.

No one will miss me back on Earth, at least not for a while, because I was mostly on my own and had no close friends and few associates that had any significant contact with me. My parents are both alive and live in a large city in another state and remain incommunicado (we don't talk much).

I didn't get along with my mom or dad very well during my teenage years, and then, life got in the way; I joined the army, and after being discharged, I was too busy with other things to try and mend my differences with them. My mother called me occasionally, to see if I was still alive and to wish me well. Other than that, we had little meaningful conversations. My father was as stubborn as I was and didn't find the time or make the time to reach out to me. Now, the time and opportunity for making amends has passed, and I have my regrets.

Siblings, consisted of one brother, younger than me by two years, and a sister, three years older than me. They are both married and busy with their lives and taking care of my two nephews, sons of my sister, and one niece, the daughter of my younger brother. Whom keep their grandparents (my parents) proud and occupied. And that makes me glad. I got along with both of my siblings but didn't stay in contact after I moved out of state. They have their lives, and I have mine. And now I have my regrets with them also, about not making more of an effort at keeping in touch and participating in their lives more often than I did.

My whole family lived in the same city, the one I moved away from before joining the army. And after my military tour ended, I didn't go back home and try to mend the fences with my parents. I was the black sheep of the family, due mostly to being young and naive. My family did send me Hallmark cards during my birthdays and greeting cards during the holidays, to keep me up-to-speed about family events and gatherings that I missed. I had hoped to make amends one day, but that day never came, and now, I might never have the chance to reach out to my parents, my siblings, nephews, and niece.

It seemed at times as if I was alone on the tiny and cramped Alien ship. Tiny, because it appeared small with only a winding passage (corridor), with little elbow room to stretch out. I was unaware of other humans or alien entities other than the occasional darting shadows of something that I couldn't make out. I wondered where or how anything other than me could fit if they or it were on the ship with me.

The ship was closing in on me. But there had to be more ship somewhere in the bizarre Alien craft to make it practical. I hadn't seen anyone or anything besides the shadow, which could have been my own shadow. The available space on the ship excluded room to hide, and almost too tight for an Alien or goblin to fit in there with me. I didn't feel alone in my small capsule. There was an overpowering inexplicable energy in the air of the kind one feels at large gatherings and wild parties; whatever it was, remained out of my comprehensive field of view and awareness.

Some creature or thing, human or otherwise, pulled me out of my house during the storm and placed me inside of the Alien ship. That was a forgone conclusion in my mind since I certainly didn't fly up to the ship on my accord. I didn't even know that there was an Alien ship parked above my house. And had I seen a UFO parked above my house, I would have totally freaked out. For some god-only-knows reason, something plucked me from my home and placed me inside this sardine can. I kept telling myself that I should be in a panic. I'm inside of a fucking Alien ship abducted by god damn incognito and invisible freaking Space Aliens!

Meandering endlessly, since I found myself on the ship, I knew I had to be nearing something revelatory about my situation. I stopped walking and peered out of one of the peculiar apertures, orifices, portholes or whatever they are that blinked into existence whenever I stopped or moved forward, as a kind of obscure incentive to keep me moving forward, I presumed. When I retraced my steps, or tried to move backward, the portholes hid out of my sight and became nonexistent. When that happened, it was like I was in a small dark closet. Lights dimmed and then went out completely if I persisted in backing up to return to where I first found myself on the ship. I tried more than once to go back, and the brutal darkness that ensued sent shivers and chills up and down my spine. I was so afraid that I'm sure my hair stood straight up all over my head and neck like the quills of a porcupine. It was creepy and eerie as hell. I've never experienced such horrid fear in my life, not even when bullets were coming in my direction and crackling around me during my army days. It was freaky and unnerving that the ship had me moving forward and further into the abyss with no way of turning back.

Looking out the windows that periodically changed shape and size when they blinked into view I could tell that the ship was traveling through space at enormous speed. Space particles the size of grains of sand, outside the ship, lit up as they shot past the ship. I saw the blue hue of Earth in full retreat, as the planet continued to shrink and be left in the cosmic dust, as the ship sped further and further away. Small objects, particles of space matter, dust, rocks, asteroids or other strange cosmic material flared up, fired up and did strange things as the ship moved furiously faster and created a wormhole through the space it shot through. The numerous sparks flying all over the place around the outer skin of the ship reminded me of a massive barrage of tracer rounds from a holocaust of machine gun fire, from one of the battles during my deployment days. It was quite the cosmic show, both inside and outside of that magical/horrific mystery tour of the Alien ship!

While gazing, and gawking in endless profound wonder out the porthole windows, it suddenly dawned on me that I must be in a dream and dreaming this whole damn Alien thing up. "I had to be dreaming," I thought to myself. There was no other rational explanation that I could think of at that moment that could explain, in any meaningful way, my experience. My maddening calmness and the Alice in Wonderland scenario were far too strange, too fantastical and too bizarre, to be real. It was no ordinary dream, if that is what it was. I was more awake and aware and excited beyond reason, while inside of that tin can, than I ever was or could ever be when I was awake, back on earth, about anything.

I avoided the drug scene and seldom drank beer, wine or whiskey, and certainly hadn't drunk anything that night, before the storm hit. I didn't have any booze in the house to drink, had I wanted to. I rarely invited people over to my house, so I had no stash of the bubbly to serve up to friends, or dip into on lonely and boring nights. I was a bit of a paranoid eccentric, thinking that anyone I invited over might come back when I wasn't home and steal my stuff. Not that I had a whole lot of stuff worth stealing, other than my tools, a computer, and television, which were my main assets besides my house and land.

I had no close and trusty friends, and therefore, everyone was a suspect. I attributed my paranoia to living out in the boonies and being exposed to the whims of criminals who were forever on the prowl and looking for easy opportunities when no one was home. Robberies and break-ins were common out in the sticks. Therefore, my paranoid distrust of people wasn't completely unreasonable. However, I had never been robbed, or my house ransacked, as was the case for some of my farmer neighbors. Probably due to my working from home a lot and all the precautions I took when I wasn't home and in the field doing jobs.

I had thought about getting a dog to guard my property and my house, and for the added benefit of companionship. I only had a few neighbors, and the nearest one lived about a mile or more away from my place. I was all alone at my creaky and spooky old house out in the backwoods, where I was serenaded nightly by all kinds of primordial animal and insect sounds, and the howls from mysterious creatures coming from the back of my house, from deep in the thick dark timber. The freaky noises and the hungry mosquitoes are partly to blame for my lack of sitting on the front porch and star gazing on lazy summer nights. Stargazing is the one thing I wished I had done more while on Earth now that I'm out among the stars perhaps for good.

Living in the boondocks was quite a life change for a city boy as I was. I became a lot more independent while in the army, otherwise, I would have remained a city slicker and never moved to such an isolated homestead in the murky woods. In the city, I understood the rules and ways of the streets more than I did about what strange creatures prowling in the woods, especially during the night. As far as getting a pet for companionship and to guard my property, I never owned a pet in my life and didn't want to be bogged down with one, knowing how needy and attention hogs they can be. My brother has a dog, and the few times I went to visit him the dog was all over me, wanting to play, which I did. Life kept me plenty busy, and I didn't have the required energy or time to take care of a dog's enormous needs for affection, so I nixed the man's best friend idea whenever it crept into my mind.

I had an old pistol that I inherited from my grandfather, but I never shot it and didn't know if it worked. I considered buying a shotgun for protection, just never got around to it due to finances and other priorities for my money.

Superstition, the paranormal and religious stuff, rarely entered my mind and I gave such ideas little credence during my time on Earth. My parents were religious (somewhat); they believed in a higher power; an old man with a beard that they and many other people called God. They didn't believe wholeheartedly in practicing their beliefs, and rarely attended church to worship as they once did when I was growing up, and the whole family went to church. I never felt anything for the religion they preached, even early on when they were serious about their faith, and I was young and impressionable. At an early age, I was unenthusiastic with religious stories, and as I matured, I figured everyone created their heaven and hell on earth. I believed that way until my abduction. Now I'm not sure what to believe.

Moments before my abduction I had finished eating a hamburger that I picked up in the small town that was about five miles from my home. I was in a hurry to get back to my house to watch one of my favorite shows on my big screen television and used the drive-through window at one of the fast-food restaurants I regularly patronized. The young woman at the pickup window who took my order was new. I had never seen her before; she was friendly, more so than some of the others that worked at the restaurant. She was cute, and I nearly asked her out for a date. But as luck had it, the cars behind me, also in a rush to pick up food and get home, were piling up behind me, which caused me to move out of the way as soon as I received my food. I planned on going back another day and asking her out. Not a likely prospect at this point in my life.

Transfixed with cosmic scenery going on outside the window of the ship, I hesitated to place my focus back into the ship, which was equally stupendous and, also, flirted with me for my full attention, with its brazen marquee-like displays on the interior walls that swathed snugly around me like a bundled child on a cold, frigid night. Still, I didn't want to miss the remarkable spectacles and surprises from the space fairies outside the window, if that was what some of the weird things I saw out the porthole were. I was on a constant lookout for the bizarre happenings that popped into view and just as quickly flared out of view.

Marveling and guessing what it was I saw, planets, moons, other alien spacecraft or any number of magical and supernatural wonders that appeared as whimsical spectators, and watching me from outside the ship and sneaking peeks and giggling at me through the portholes left me rapt. Extremely unnerving seeing such strange creatures on the other side of the glass, near enough for them to reach through the glass and touch or grab me. Had it not been for the mellow state of mind keeping me calm I don't know what I would have done.

The peculiar spectators tagging alongside the ship and clearly visible outside the porthole, preoccupied much of my time with endless wonder rather than terror. I marveled at their abilities to keep up with a ship which was moving at mindboggling fantastical speeds, so much so, that a cocoon of cosmic material formed around the glowing ship.

The creatures outside the window of the ship were pure amazing and friendly, like cute and "animated" stuffed teddy bears, waving at me, then hiding from me like children playing hide and seek. At this point, I was ready and willing to believe in the tooth fairy, Santa Claus, and the Easter bunny. God, damn it, I've seen so much crazier shit than those childhood fairy tales combined on the ship and outside the porthole windows, enough to fill dozens of children's books or horror books, if I was so inclined to write it all down!

I don't recall ever being so flighty back on Earth as I seem to be now, clutched by wonderment on one level and sheer terror on another level. There were very few things, if anything, that I believed in or placed my trust wholeheartedly into when I was a lost and clueless soul concerning the paranormal and Space Aliens, back on planet Earth. Still, the unknown elements of existence that filtered into my awareness, made space and everything else I could get my head around nothing less than remarkably amazing and mesmerizing. Whatever types of entities, beings, fairies and other paranormal critters flying around the ship, as if escorting us to that far-flung planet or place, left me drooling, intrigued and speechless.

Strange creatures of inconceivable appearances and looks orbited around the ship inside their tiny craft and some without craft, accompanied the ship as we sped along our merry way through space and towards the cosmic nut-house. Where, I was sure, I belonged.

I didn't know much about cosmology, space and the cosmos in general before my abduction and I remain ignorant of that still. The celestial stuff like comets, stars, quasars, Black Holes, galaxies, and the universe, other than the few things I picked up in grade school, and from the occasional news reports from NASA's missions and probes, during my adult years, remained mysteries. Had I known (remembered) how fantastic and mind-expanding space is, I would have spent more time learning all I could about the cosmos. Earth is nothing more than a grain of sand, a speck in an endless ocean filled to the brim with strange, bizarre and delightful cosmological life. Stranger, and diversely populated with enormous varieties of life than the billions of types of marine life in the seas and the oceans back on Earth. I didn't consciously observe billions of space creatures, or perhaps I did, considering the hugeness of space and all the unidentifiable things I saw out the porthole window.

From the creaky porch of my old farmhouse on a clear night, the stars covered and lit up the night sky like a blanket of horny fireflies searching for romantic flings with other horny fireflies, metaphorically speaking. The stars and the planets certainly didn't dance around the sky like fireflies, but I draw that comparison because the fireflies did dance around my yard and fascinated me more than the stars above, until the mosquitoes ran me indoors. Nevertheless, in the boondocks, the stars were real, robust and plump in the night sky, boasting majestically about their magnificent beauty. Nothing short of pure eye-candy for those who took the time to look up at the flirty and naughty night sky. A sky that was fully intent on seducing human minds and forcing ecstasy on the human neurons and all the accompanying senses. Unlike when I lived in the big city, with all its light haze that botched and blocked the wimpy stars from view. The little I saw of the stars while living in the big city didn't manage to capture much of my interest or imagination.

Regretfully, during the time I lived in the country and was blessed with spectacular nightly views of the heavens, I seldom sat down on the one chair on the porch to consider the mysterious universe and the wonders it held and hid from us, mere mortals. I had more important things to keep me grounded; fishing, hunting and finding ways to pay the bills with the least amount of work. All poor excuses and lost opportunities to marvel at the free and greatest show Earthlings will ever have while alive on Earth.

At times, I was laid back and far too lazy for my own good. Most times, I was industrious and kept myself busy doing things I liked doing. Construction work is what I loved doing, gazing up at the stars on clear nights, not so much. I blame it on the crick in my neck and the biting insects.

Spiraling further into the belly of the beast, my circular descent down or up the lengthy and drawn-out ship's corridor, perceptivity narrowed even more. The hall got smaller and seemed to be closing around me and became skin tight at places. Still, I observed and marveled at the overwhelming number of alien designs that played on the walls, floor, and ceilings, that were now on and inside my skin, like griffins teasing me to pick up my pace and the speed of my stride to Hell?

The alien graffiti covering the surface areas of the ship, and me too, became restless and edgy at the least bit of hesitation displayed by me. I only stopped to collect my wits and attempt to wrangle some sense out of what was happening to me. I stopped and sneaked a peek through the hypnotic portholes, because stopping made the holes come alive and into focus from their blurred and invisible state. I peeked out the windows every so often to regain and maintain the feeling that everything was real and normal and to keep my mind from caving in on me. Space was real; it was the one thing that looked unchanged from when I did manage to look up at the stars back on Earth from my little plot in the boonies.

When I attempted to turn back fearing what lay ahead, mysterious figures on the walls and strange lights flickered warnings not to look back but to look and keep moving forward. Like a child in a funhouse filled with strange and confusing mirrors on the walls, moving forward was daunting, perplexing and like walking through a "mind" field of surprises. Completely lost inside the freak show, I heeded the signs when I understood them and voyaged onward.

I began spinning deeper into the hole as the corridor continued to tighten around me, squeezing me like toothpaste out of a tube, and then, like water in a bathtub swirling down the drain at the end of the tunnel, the corridor, the passageway, vanished. I dropped into another part of the ship and landed on my head on the floor below with my legs up in the air. I was free from the confining intestinal track of the ship. But I was upside down and so was everything in the ship. I must have hit my head hard when I fell out of the tube, though the fall didn't hurt and I felt nothing out of the ordinary. Except, nothing ordinary inside that ship. Upside down was now my new perspective and, as I began walking, everything became normal again, whatever normal was now.

I found myself inside of a large expansive room, area, space, cavern, perhaps a very large maze inside of the cavern. I could walk in any direction without restraint or taunting by animated graffiti that flashed and flickered from every pixeled-covered surface lining the tube-like passageway that had become my skin.

The inside of that part of the ship was immense; I had no idea a UFO could be so huge, so large and massive. From the pictures (real or fake) that I've seen of UFOs on the covers of tabloid magazines at the grocery store checkout, they looked rather small and insignificant like a frisbee that is thrown into the air. I never saw the outside of the UFO that I was inside of now. I didn't see the UFO when I was looking out of my window when at my house during the storm. It was dark and bleak outside, with torrents of rain hitting the window pane, which blocked my view of the sky and made it near impossible to see anything other than the thrashing of trees. I was trying to see if a tornado was barreling down on my house, and I did step out the door for a better look and was nearly drenched and blown away by the torrents of rain and strong winds. The way the house shook I thought that there had to be a tornado hidden in the darkness and coming for me and my house. I was about to run down to the basement for cover when I found myself inside the UFO, instead.

I wondered too, if perhaps I had died during the storm and was now a ghost on my way to heaven, hopefully, and not hell, which I would have thought was in the other direction, down. In truth, I didn't know up from down at that point.

The UFO was up and above my house, but I've been on a downward spiral since the moment I found myself inside the alien contraption, but was never sure. The house looked intact from where I viewed it from the UFO window. So, the house didn't get hit by a tornado. I didn't see a tornado from my perch on the ship when I looked down from the clouds. In my urgency to flee to safety, I could have fallen down the steps into my dark and musty basement and broken my neck. If so, I had no recollection of the fall. I felt fine, way better than I ever have and my body seemed undamaged and whole.

From the great hall in the bowels of the ship, I did what I did when I first found myself a giddy prisoner inside this flying funhouse; I enthusiastically explored the vast new surroundings inside the cavern. Choice of direction didn't matter as it did in the corridor. No animated symbols spurred me in any direction, and no portholes made themselves known to me, which I instantly missed the wonderful and relaxing feeling I had from looking out into the vastness of magical space.

The portholes vanished completely, and I found no new ones in this part of the ship. I could've sat down on the floor or the ceiling and waited for Alien creatures to hunt me down and do whatever it is Alien creatures do to their human prey, but I didn't, nor did I want to sit and wait. Gravity existed on the ship and held me down or up. Where my feet were, is where the floor was that held me in place and provided me with equilibrium. I didn't float around like the astronauts do inside the space station.

I had energy and curiosity enough to explore for eternity. I plowed forward with ever increasing hunger for whatever mysteries lay ahead for me to find and crack. For the most part, I had little or no fear on the ship; nevertheless, plenty of things gave me the willies, but I could not head for the exit on this ship even if I knew where the exit was. Being out in space was now my prison. I had no desire to find an exit or leave this ship due to the thrills and fun bestowed upon me by whoever owned the ship.

"What horrendous creatures lay in wait to pounce and insert their Alien spawn into my virgin human body", was on the backburner of my mind. I am no virgin and had my share of dalliances with girls from a very early age and more so while in high school. But I am new, a virgin to the Alien craze that has infected much of human thought in the science fiction genre of books and movies. A fiction that has abruptly turned into reality for me and that now dominates every moment, as I voraciously explore the cosmic mystery entrenched inside my soul.

I remember the "Alien" movies with Sigourney Weaver and that unstoppable, petrifying alien creature chasing her all over the universe. But it was only a movie. I did go to movies with girlfriends for the most obvious of reasons, to make out. The creepier the movie, the sooner our bodies merged and became as one, more so on cool autumn nights at the outdoor drive-in theater in the backseat of my first car that my dad bought for me.

Now that I'm inside of a real Alien ship, there must be real Alien creatures scurrying around somewhere inside of it. They, or it, needed to stop by and introduce themselves and bring my mind to rest. I'm not bothered much by the occasional alarm bells going off in my head and warning me of potential danger from the mysterious Devils remaining out of sight, excepting their sporadic shadows. I'm for the most part, calm, in a ship filled with potential nightmarish suspense, a contradiction I was acutely aware of. Even little moments of serenity were too much for someone trapped inside the belly of an Alien ship! So, the occasional alarm bells going off in my head brought some reality into focus.

Inside the ship was mysteriously quiet, I couldn't hear my footsteps as I walked across the metallic looking floor, though it didn't feel metallic walking on it. Soft and almost slippery the floor was that I felt I could glide over the floor with little effort. I assumed my hearing was unaffected and was probably keen as were all my other bodily physical senses, sight, touch, taste, smell; however, I detected no scents or odors since my encounter with the Alien craft and had no occasions to test my taste buds.

POOL

I came upon a circular pool filled with what looked like plain water. From my alien-ship-skewed mind, the water didn't appear deep, perhaps a little over knee-high, I estimated. The water, or unknown liquid, was clear when I first approached the pool, but soon changed and became cloudy as I stood near it. The pool was about three to four hundred feet in circumference, and the liquid in it was motionless like a sheet of metal and reflected like a mirror even though it was cloudy. I could see my reflection clearly as it rose from the liquid and looked at me from above the water. It was a damn good and accurate representation of me, almost like a clone levitating above the water and mimicking my every move. My awareness of me standing there looking at myself created an element of creepiness that washed over me like a bucket of super cold ice water thrown over me. It took some quick mind adjustment to keep me calm, collected and stop my shivering. My fear genes, apparently got turned down a few notches by someone or something, moments after my body and mind were sucked off the Earth and absorbed into the cosmic vessel. Otherwise, some serious panic would have overtaken me.

I attempted to touch the clone or image, and my hand passed through it. I thought to myself, "hologram, not a clone." Big relief swept over me, or else I might have lost it. The alien liquid from the pool projecting out of the water created my reflection similar to a hologram, and then swiftly vanished soon after I touched it bursting like a life-sized soap bubble.

A strong impulse came over me to place my hand into the liquid in the pool, and I did and withdrew my hand quickly, and my hand was not wet. I still had a hand, so it wasn't Alien acid and certainly wasn't water. The liquid was neither hot nor cold; it was a perfect temperature similar and equal to the air temperature in that room, which was comfortable.

Visibility inside the ship was queer and unusual and changed often. I could see very clearly most of the time, but at some point, and at sometimes, the rest of the ship became draped and shrouded in mystifying fog. A haze surrounded the pool of liquid and appeared to rise out of or percolate from the pool that formed into a light mist. The liquid emitted a strange bluish vapor but had no odor or smell as would be the case at an indoor pool back on earth (strong chlorine odor). The fog parted whenever I walked allowing me to see a few feet of what was in front of me and closed behind me as I passed.

The liquid in the pool had a mind, and the mind seemed to call to me with strange messages that appeared in my mind that invited me to step into its placid water. It was foolish to do so without knowing what the liquid was, yet, I didn't hesitate. I disrobed and stepped into the liquid and lowered my body into it slowly. It was about four feet deep, far deeper than I first guesstimated. I stretched out and floated on my back on top of the buoyant liquid. I turned over and plunged into the water and discovered I could breathe while submerged in the liquid. With my eyes fully opened, I could see clearly with no burning sensation, unlike when I swam at public pools the chlorine burned my eyes. Submerged in the pool the liquid was not cloudy but tremendously clear. There was nothing to see in the pool only the circular walls of the pool, which were a plain white color with no designs or animated Alien graffiti.

After a time of floating on the liquid, I got out of the pool and put my clothing back on. It was strange that I didn't drip and needed no towel to dry. I was certain I would be back for another dip because it was stimulating and relaxing and it caused me to dream while I was awake. In one of the dreams, I was told by a person, a humanoid of some type, to leave the pool and return later. I missed the soothing and enchanted liquid instantly the moment I got out. I wanted more answers about the ship and why I was on it and continued my journey through the maze searching for the answers to questions I had on my mind while dreaming in the pool. Little knowing at the time that the pool held many, if not all the answers to the cosmic mysteries within its supernatural waters.

In one of my dreams, while fully awake and drifting on the surface of the pool waters, animals talked to me like people talk. I was in a world of beasts and creatures of the kind I saw as a child visiting the zoo with my siblings and parents. Many other types of animals that I haven't seen on Earth also were in that same dream, and we chatted back and forth about the strangest of things. The animals were not wild but civilized and had the same desires and feelings as humans on planet Earth had. They lived in houses and apartments and had jobs, careers and ran businesses just like humans. Some were nice and talked with me as equals in the animal kingdom, others snapped at me and cast insults at the "ape-man," as they referred to me in the dream. The whole dream wasn't normal, as most dreams are not normal, they are fractured remnants of daily activities, and that's how I treated the dream, strange and confusing, and little more.

But I didn't exist in a "normal" world anymore; I was now living in a land where myths were real and normal. Alice in Wonderland, a book that one of my teachers read to me and my class in elementary school and a movie my parents took my siblings and me to once, didn't much interest me at the time. I never gave the movie or book much thought, and truthfully, I didn't care for that fable or many other tales of my youth. Now, I find myself trapped inside the insane world of fairytales. Soon enough, I discovered that some fairytales are nightmares.

While in the pool, I was told many things that made little or no sense to me at the time. One thing that stuck in my mind was that time doesn't exist on the ship, but the ship exists in time. The strange animal that told me that, also told me I would understand what that means before my voyage in the ship ended. That was such a confusing statement and concept that I could hardly believe I would ever unravel the meaning.

Probing in the house of mirrors that the Alien ship was, led me to a room, a smaller room inside the larger area that I first entered before taking a dip in the pool. The room was empty and had other egresses (doors, openings) that led to other rooms and passageways. I didn't stop to count the number of exits, and I walked through one of the openings, the nearest one to me and entered a short hallway. Several openings (doors) were attached to the hallway and rather than take the nearest one I went to an opening in the center of the hall and passed into another room.

To my shocking surprise inside the room were four humans like me, standing in the room, two men and two women all looked about the same age as me. No one was talking, and they each seemed lost in their little worlds and without cares or concerns. Excited about finding other people on the ship, I spoke and said, "Hello." Fully expecting a "Hello" or "hi" back from the four people. No one in the room was listening and acted as if they didn't hear me, and ignored my presence like I was not in the room with them. I said "Hello" several more times and no response whatsoever. It was not a language thing because even if none of the people in the room spoke English, they still would have acknowledged me in some way but did not. Nevertheless, relief came over me knowing that I was not the only human on the ship. It mattered little that the four humans were in a zombie daze, which I expected, being they were trapped inside of a mind-scrambling UFO, as was I.

The people in the room were not manikins, they moved around, fidgeted and walked in and out of the room while I was there, and watching their every move, action and reaction to my inquiries, turned interrogations. To my disappointment and consternation, their responses remained the same, nothing worthwhile; none of the four answered any of my questions or reacted in any way to anything I said to them. The movements they made included glancing at their wrist watches as if they were waiting for someone or something to show up.

I went up close to one of the men for a better look at his watch to see what time it had stopped. Like my watch, his second hand was not moving, and I noticed that the time on his watch was later than the time that was on my watch. I surmised he was picked up after I was and entered the ship about two hours later than I. Which meant I was on the ship at least two hours (assuming he was from the same time zone as me). Why I hadn't run into him or the others sooner, puzzled me. I did the same with the other three, looked at their watches, and concluded I had been on the ship four hours or more, if we were from the same time zone. There was no way for me to know what time zone they came from without me getting personal and lifting wallets and peering into purses and checking drivers' licenses and some other ID if I didn't find a drivers' license. I did my search and astonishingly encountered no resistance from any of the four people in the room (something very strange about that). Turned out they were all from the same time zone as me, Midwest. That boggled my mind. It didn't feel like I had been away from my house and my planet that long!

I was neither angered, scared or frustrated by that revelation and conundrum, perhaps due to the pleasurable moments I also experienced, that took my mind away from the negatives. I grabbed one of the men by the shoulders and shook him hard hoping to ignite a response from him. Nothing came of it. He simply continued going through the motions, as before I grabbed and shook him. I wondered why they were in a group of four and I was alone by myself. I would have preferred bouncing around the ship with other humans in the same predicament as I, had I the choice. Then again, I was a loner back on Earth by choice. Curiously, the four in the room were not communicating with each other and appeared oblivious to each other as they were of me. Things were not as they seemed on the ship, so it was possible that I was the one that was off kilter and out of sync and out of touch with them.

I hadn't seen an opening (window) to the outside world since I fell into the labyrinth from the original hallway. I couldn't tell if I was still inside the UFO flying through space or if I had been transported to some other place, ship or building on some planet, moon or space city. I didn't feel any motion as if on a moving ship. Perhaps, I was in a padded cell in some loony bin back on Earth, drugged up to the point that I couldn't feel reality anymore, only peace and tranquility from the drugs administered to me by the doctors at the sanitarium. It was difficult to be upset or paranoid when your mind and body are in a state of ecstasy as I was.

Giddy, and happy as hell, and feeling downright marvelous, described perfectly how I felt. It didn't add up, or maybe it did. I didn't miss my house, my life back on Earth, my job and responsibilities or my family. I loved my family, but I did not miss them. I didn't have anything important going on that needed my attention back on Earth, not that I would have been bothered if I had. I was between jobs, recently having finished building a deck on a new house for a builder acquaintance of mine, and was taking it easy, spending more time fishing and doing minor repairs around my house that I had put on hold. Now I wasn't sure I would ever see my house or family again and wasn't sure I wanted to. That thought should have depressed me and deflated my over-inflated giddiness that plagued me, but it didn't.

I was ok with whatever was happening to me since the moment I set foot on this alien happy-machine. I had no real fear that the Aliens were going to eat me alive or inject me with monstrous Alien spawn. I was optimistic that things were going to be fun and interesting and be the wonderful stories I would tell my grandkids someday if I ever have children and grandchildren.

The four people I had run into were probably in the same situation as I was, giddy, lost and confused inside their heads and unable to express their feelings or themselves to the other people around them. For some reason, we were not allowed to communicate with each other about our strange experiences by whoever abducted and imprisoned us on the Alien craft.

I presumed that we were on our way to some other planet for relocation purposes, perhaps some human-Alien exchange program that the Aliens worked out with the governments of Earth, as often claimed by conspiracy theorists around the world. I didn't read much of the conspiracy stuff about Aliens visiting Earth, but friends of mine did, and it came out in conversations when they were drinking or high on weed at some Friday night party I attended infrequently.

I was the one who rolled my eyes when the talk turned to Aliens abducting people or that the governments around the world were in cahoots with space beings and trading gold and other earth resources in exchange for human slaves, food or biological stuff that the Aliens needed for their survival. Or we, the captured five humans on the ship, were part of a technology exchange with the Aliens so that humans can drive around town with their heads up their asses while texting or talking on technological Alien marvels like "smartphones." I know now without a doubt that my buddies back on Earth weren't far off their rockers after all.

That was the only thing that was certain in my mind so far, Aliens did, in fact, abduct me. Humans certainly didn't have the kind of magical technology that was inside of this ship, that I was aware. Whether what was happening to me and the other humans on the ship was part of some covert government scheme, I might never know. We were on a spaceship and flying somewhere, some place out in the cosmic boondocks and by now had to be untold gazillions of miles from planet Earth.

Some parts of the ship were lit up and so bright it was like being inside of a surgical operating room. Everything was crystal clear when not in the fog that ebbed and flowed around the great labyrinth inside the Alien vessel. A few places were completely shrouded in thick fog and other places not as much. Nevertheless, I could see without much difficulty while in that room, every detail of my hands as if they were under a microscope. My veins and the miniscule dirt particles lodged inside skin crevices, and under my fingernails. I never noticed how filthy my hands and my whole body were until now. The grimy dirt covering my skin, head to toe, grossed me out and made me want to shower and scrub my whole body with a Brillo pad. Things like that, that exploded microscopic details into large, easy-to-view objects without the help of a magnifying glass or other devices, made me wonder if my mind had succumbed to an LSD trip.

The punks that worked at the drive-through restaurant that I once or twice had a minor run-in, could have spiked my food or drink with drugs. A hallucination caused by acid, crack, LSD or any number of hallucinogenic mind-altering drugs would explain the things I'm now seeing and experiencing. I could be passed out on my bed or the floor of my house and believing that I'm on some crazy-ass Alien space ship. That seemed logical and something those two guys were underhanded enough to do. I would not put it past them tampering with my food for laughs. But them wasting drugs on me wasn't likely. They didn't have a lot of money, and once asked to borrow money from me. Jokingly, I asked them if I looked like a bank or a sucker and that, inadvertently ended whatever friendship we might have had.

The dirt on my hands and the rest of me bothered me even if it was only noticeable under the extreme light of that one room in the ship. I worked hard and got plenty dirty doing jobs back on Earth, but I was a firm believer that 'cleanliness is next door to godliness.' I was kind of fanatical about hygiene and had a strong belief in keeping myself clean. Godliness was a whole other story, being I was an atheist and had my share of culpabilities. I was no saint, and now it appeared true, I was unclean. I learned soon enough that I was not filthy, but something more bizarre was happening to my body and to my mind while being distracted by the bizarre things going on in the ship.

I felt no motion from the ship's movement through space the whole time I was on the craft. When I was in the corridor, I could see motion from the portholes, though I didn't feel anything, no movement in the ship. Now in the great hall of the ship, I had no indication of motion since there were no portholes to get a view of what was going on outside the ship, no windows and no egress of any kind to the outside. Which normally would have been bothersome to me, being I was claustrophobic back on Earth. My time and duration through the narrow corridor should have done me in because of that phobia; instead, my journey through the restrictive tunnel was pleasant and overall enjoyable.

I hadn't had any real fears or phobias on the ship even when the hallway closed in around me towards the end before spitting me out into the grand ballroom that I am now in. There was no way of knowing if we were still traveling through space or had arrived at our destination, wherever that destination might be. Like a child stuck inside of a car on a long trip, I wanted to know if we were "there yet." I enjoyed exploring the ship and, in many ways, dreaded arriving at our destination and the fun coming to an end. I also could hardly contain my excitement of reaching a distant and exotic planet with strange and wonderful places to relish and explore.

I began to visualize what it would be like to set foot on another planet, assuming I get out of this Alien container alive. My mind flooded with ideas and possibilities about strange beings and magnificent cities where all people lived in peace, joy, and happiness, forever after (I didn't take the slave trade/exchange idea seriously). The destination had to be a wonderful place, if the ship was any indication of their fanciful abilities and mind-expanding technologies, not to mention the level of peacefulness I now felt, like I have never experienced before in my life, nor did I think such things possible or lasting.

It appeared as if I didn't need food or drink because I haven't had either for several hours or longer, based on the wristwatches of the people in that one room. I had gone longer without food and drink during military operations and even when I worked on constructions projects far from civilization out in the sticks on a farmer's house or barn and hadn't packed sufficient food supplies to carry me through the completion of the job. I was always hungry and thirsty and therefore made sure (most of the time) that I had plenty of food and drinks on hand. On the ship, I had no appetite for food or thirst for drinks, which made no sense to me whatsoever.

That was biologically contrary to my human needs, desires and wants back on Earth. Such peculiar situations and paradoxes on the ship kept me wondering if I was alive, dead or in a dream state inside of a comatose body in some hospital, mental institution, city morgue or funeral parlor. Supposing I was not already embalmed and entombed inside a fancy casket, buried six feet down in a cemetery of my parent's choosing.

ALIEN TUBES

I continued exploring the labyrinth of twists and turns and came upon yet another mysterious chamber. The most mysterious by far, and that glowed with the illumination of electrified plasma. The chamber had many large glass tubes that stood floor to ceiling and filled with a colorful semiliquid gelatin type of solution or material and covered in a volatile electric field. The material inside the tubes may have been stable and not volatile, but to me, it looked dangerous and ready to blow the whole ship to pieces with all the bubbly and electrical sparks going on inside the tubes. The room was crammed full of the electrified tubes bubbling and throwing off sparks like a thunderstorm on steroids.

The tubes contained, within the strange-looking dynamic and glowing-hot solution, naked humans, suspended inside the viscous matter. The human bodies had to be cooked with all that radiation going on around and through the bodies. The sight of such brutality reeked of violently cruel inhumanity against human beings. And I was a god damned human being, the same as all the humans inside the jars! I remained calm and didn't want to go into panic mode and lose my composure, and tried to make sense of what now confronted me and confounded my unraveling mind. There had to be a good explanation, or I was in big trouble, being I was a prisoner in that madhouse of an Alien horror ship.

One human body was inside each of the electrified glowing glass containers. Wires and tubes and other types of bizarre apparatus were attached to various body orifices and directly on the skin of the humans in each glass tube. The eerie monstrosity of the tubes presumably represented an Alien-type of life support system; or some other perverse Alien experimentation with human bodies and their anatomies. Soon after viewing the very disturbing Alien setup, I became physically ill and wanted to run and get away from that place in the ship and the ship itself. But I knew, down deep inside, there was no leaving or escaping the infernal Alien ship that somehow now owned me.

Shaken to the point of losing my mind and the tranquility that had kept my mind afloat up until I stumbled into that nightmare, I walked deeper into the nightmare rather than run from it. I struggled with my calmness more than the shock of what was in that room, which wasn't normal, at least not for me and not under those kinds of circumstances. Nevertheless, after the initial shock, I discovered that I was ok with the incredible bizarreness in that Alien laboratory or Alien butcher shop. Whatever it was, it wasn't usual, it was a Frankenstein-laboratory setup that didn't quite fit in with the crazy shit I had thus far experienced in Alien-Ville.

The room was large, and the tubes evenly spaced about five feet apart from each other in every direction. That place, that room was lit up and bright and near blinding, like looking directly into the sun. My eyes adjusted quickly and everything was clear and gruesome. There was no fog or mist in that room, and every detail of the human bodies in the man-sized jars was easily and disgustingly viewable.

Such clarity, made looking at the humans so much more outrageous, every detail and every skin-crevasse could be seen far better than if under a microscope. So much information, too much for me to appreciate, being I was not in the medical field or a mortician. For med students, doctors, nurses, scientists, and undertakers, the detailed human anatomy of the people in the jars would be a treasure trove of phenomenally helpful information about human biology. But with the risk of singed hair, from all the electrical sparks flying around the room and surrounding each tube and the bodies inside the glass structures.

Had I been on earth and walked into such a place I would have run out screaming in horror. But I was inside of an Alien spaceship and breathing air that was keeping me happy and calm for the most part. I didn't know if the sedative was administered through the air or by some other means that kept me comfortably numb.

I calmly walked around and took a closer look at the people stuffed inside the saturated-with-plasma, tubes. The facial expressions of all the people I looked at seemed normal or blissful and not distressed as if in pain or horrified. There were equal numbers of men and women inside the tubes. Perhaps they were being pumped with feel good drugs intravenously from all the tubing and wiring protruding from various places on their bodies. I didn't recognize any of the hundred in that room but soon discovered that there were other such rooms or chambers with similar people and wires and tubes dangling and sticking out from their mouths, noses, and anuses, too. A distressing and revolting sight that I could not get used to seeing, even in my happy state of mind!

My curiosity propelled me to look closer at some of the tube-enclosed people in the other rooms, since I had nothing else to do but look for clues to what this ship was all about. It certainly wasn't a sexual thing on my part, due to the fact there was nothing sexually provocative about viewing pickled naked humans with amplified flaws and other bodily details inside large glass jars. I assumed the people were alive, otherwise why bother with keeping them inside the jars and pumping fluids through them along with the massive doses of electrical shock therapy. I wondered if I was going to end up inside one of them jars as well. I hadn't run into any empty jars to that point, but the ship seemed infinite with unbelievable numbers of rooms and spaces that I had yet to explore.

During further inspections of the tubes, I noticed that one of the bodies in one of the laboratories looked familiar. I racked my brain to remember who this person was and when and where I had seen him. He was in his thirties, approximately the same age as all the people in the tubes. He wasn't anyone I knew from the small town near my house. Then my jaw dropped, I recognized him from the room with the four zombies; he was one of them or looked just like one of the men in that room. Perplexed, I decided to look for that room with the four people I ran into during my first encounter, to see if they were still there, more precisely, if he was still there, the man that was now in the glass tube. I found many rooms and some of the rooms had people in them that were also fidgeting and existing in their little worlds of seclusion and staring blankly at the walls, unaware of me and the others around them like the original four people that I found. I was aware of them, the people, they must have been aware of me on some mental level, but didn't show it.

After I retraced my steps, and combed through several rooms, I found the room I was searching for, the

original room with the two men and two women inside. The
four people were still there, doing what they were doing
when I left them earlier, absolutely nothing. The man that I
saw inside one of the tubes was in the room too, rubbing
his chin and with an expression that looked contemplative.
I grabbed him and shook him, again and again, and again,
nothing, no response from him or the other zombies in the
room. He was clothed as was everyone on the ship that I
had seen so far, except for those in the big glass jars
which were naked inside the Alien gelatin.

Perhaps it wasn't him in that tube, but someone
who looked just like him, I considered that possibility. Or,
something more sinister was at play, perhaps the tubes
were holding clones of the people on the ship. I had found
many hundreds of people in various rooms in similar
situations, predicaments, as the four in this room. I was at
a loss to understand what was happening, what was going
on. I wished that, whoever oversaw this ship or nut house,
would make themselves known to me and clear up my
confusion.

During the time that I was looking for the original
four people, I checked the watches of some of the other
people that I found milling mindlessly inside rooms. By
doing so, I discovered I had been inside the ship weeks,
perhaps many months, if not longer. I didn't check the cell
phones, assuming since my phone didn't work on the ship,

none worked. Placing my hands into the pockets of strangers didn't appeal to me, nor rummaging through women's purses for phones and IDs, but I did, and I discovered that some of the people were not from the same time zones as I was. But enough of them were for me to deduce I was on the ship a long time.

The whole time on the ship I hadn't slept a wink, at all, I should at the very least be exhausted if not sick, dying or dead. Back on earth, I needed my eight hours of sleep badly. Otherwise, I couldn't function well the rest of the day. Now, on this Alien ship and obviously and seriously deprived of any sleep whatsoever (considering the length of time I'd been on the ship), I should be severely cranky. I was never once tired and had the same energy level that I had from day one, the first day I was taken, abducted, and placed on board crazy-land-cruise lines. I hadn't eaten or drunk anything the whole time. That was impossible; I should be deceased, perhaps I was.

Then, I remembered the one dream I had while floating on top of the Alien water, and paraphrasing some unknown, invisible animal being, who told me by a voice that "time exists not inside of the ship, but the ship exists in time." Time not existing on the ship made perfect sense now and was why I was not hungry, thirsty or sleep-deprived. I was flying through "space and time" yet time was a complete illusion, a fabrication, inside this ship. Made sense for my situation but boggled my mind, which could not get around that concept of no time. I existed in a linear dimension where situations flowed nicely from one to the next. I was on the ship, then moved down or through a hall that was like a tunnel, falling into a larger area and explored endlessly through a maze of rooms, nooks, and crannies. There was a rhyme and a rhythm and progression from one situation to the next even though the whole ship was like a mad house of psychotic strangeness. I wasn't existing all bunched up, as wrapped in a straightjacket in some godforsaken corner, unable to move in a psycho ward hospital. I didn't think, but was never sure.

The ship itself was extremely pleasant to be inside. And I had no complaints about that, other than the spooky Frankenstein-laboratories that were popping out from everywhere in the ship like popcorn overflowing from a kettle and into my awareness. Colors and interesting symbols and other strange and bewitching alien motifs that had little meaning to my cognizant mind, kept me motivated, excited and distracted as I trudged along the innards of the ship of the damned. The endless drama managed to keep me entertained, enraptured and spoiled rotten, as a child in a toy store with a credit card (when petrified I should have been, from the hundreds of humans pickled in jars). I wanted more of the ship and less of the reality of what was happening inside the ship, and to my mind, body and soul (assuming I was still in possession of any of that stuff, mind, body and soul). All those pickled human beings, that was a tough one to swallow and get my mind around. I knew nothing about them and wasn't sure I wanted to know the whole story behind their terrible circumstances. Unfortunately, the two realities, or illusions, were inseparable, like a nightmare wrapped up inside of an extraordinarily pleasant dream.

It was possible that there was nothing evil going on inside the ship. I may have misinterpreted the things I saw due to the Hollywood-movie influences that have "negatized" everything we humans know about extraterrestrial Alien beings. But no food, no sleep, no water, did not compute in my puny little human brain (time or no time). Human bodies need food, water and sleep to survive and remain relevant for any length of "time"; that alone, computed. Being that I remained in my full human three-dimensional way of thinking and how I viewed stuff, even while on a ship that has disproven all my previous earthly and human ways of thinking and seeing things.

I had turned into an empty shell, slowly being drained and made devoid of my former self without realizing while it happened. I resisted confronting that reality at every turn while in the maze that shredded my mortal existence one cell at a time during every crook and turn on the long, narrow and winding path through the increasingly morbid ship.

Exploring the ship was nevertheless inspirational even with the morbid and weirdness in the mixture. It didn't matter that the ship thrashed and slashed at my every move and step by way of invisible Alien Ninjas, as I trudged along, alone. And that was the only options I had available to me thus far. Endless exploration of the mysteries hidden and lurking inside the ship, no less the hidden mysteries inside myself, propelled me to search out even more of the unknown about the ship and me. It became an addiction that I began craving. The enticing intrigue of the supernatural world, which I somehow was now and forever a part of, with no chance or choice for turning back.

I continued to people-watch (the humans in the jars) until I came upon one man inside the electrified glass tube that looked a lot like me. It could've been coincidence, I hoped and prayed. I have seen a man or two on earth that had similar facial features as my own. I studied the man inside the glass tube closely looking for other clues and noticed he had a scar exactly like what I had on my leg on his leg too (the same leg). I was scarred from an accident when I fell off my bike as a child. On seeing the scar, I shouted out, "HOLY CRAP, that is me inside that goddamned jelly jar!"

I should have, but I didn't have a brain meltdown. I didn't freak out and drop into a fetal position on the floor and suck my thumb in one of the corners in one of the many rooms on the ship. Instead, I walked to one of the other rooms where other people were standing around and felt them, grabbed one of the men and shook him, even punched him in the gut, wishing for a reaction, to see if those people were flesh and bone solid and alive. I had done that previously when I shook the two men trying for a reaction from them. I pinched myself, and I felt solid, although the pinch didn't hurt. The people I touched, shook and punched, in the ship felt solid too, we were all flesh and bone solid, yet none of them responded to my touch or my punches. "So how can we be in two places, two bodies at the same time?" I asked myself. I didn't believe a scar would show up on a clone if that's what the bodies in the pickle jars were; perhaps I was misinformed and wrong about how DNA works and what was in those jars were actual clones of all the people on the ship.

Nothing added up. I could be a ghost, I was not hungry or thirsty, and none of the other people saw me or reacted in any way towards me when I was around them, it was as if I didn't exist. I felt no pain, only happiness. But I also felt I had a physical corporal physique. I had a body and the clothes that I had on when I was first picked up by some alien being or creature from inside of this ship. Statistically, I should be filthy and rank, having gone without a shower for perhaps months. I was not smelly, in fact, I hadn't detected any odors or smells the whole time on the ship. I was not convinced that I was a ghost or spirit even when the evidence suggested that I was. I figured that, somehow, that missing time inside the ship that I heard about at the pool had something to do with much of my strange dilemma.

CONTACT

I received a summons (finally), a call inside of my mind, my head or my soul (far different from the contact I had while in the pool and inside of a dream). The first "real" contact I had since that stormy night on Earth when I had a conversation with a client on the phone minutes before the storm hit and changed everything I know about existence. Either that, or I was finally going mad and now had the proof. Voices in people's heads, minds or souls carried stigmas of psychoses, schizophrenia, and other kinds of mental illness or diseases of the mind, body, and soul.

I wasn't even sure I had a soul. I was an atheist, a non-believer that a god created the world and the universe in six days or six years or even over billions of years. Pure nonsense it was. And when I heard that the scientific community jumped on that instant-creation bandwagon with religion, and claiming that everything in the universe, including the universe itself, popped out of a speck smaller than a grain of pickling salt, from something called the "Big Bang", I had had enough, and I stopped believing in them scientists, too.

The voice in my head told me to follow the signs, flashing green arrows that instantly appeared in front of me. That was easy enough. I made many left and right turns and did a few circles and zigzags and straight lines as if I was making my way through yet another rat maze. Not much dissimilar to all the other mazes I had already walked through inside of this ship, with their mind bombs and trouser-soiling, hair-trigger, terror-inducing spins and turns. After a dizzying walk (a walk in the park, in comparison to some of my other walks in the ship), I finally reached my destination and entered the room or grotto or the pit of hell at the end of the web in the middle of the maze.

Inside the dark, creepy cavern, the walls were impregnated, encrusted with sparkling and glittering diamonds and gems of interesting colors and facets of many shapes and sizes. I walked past several types of humanoids, with animal and insect faces and full-body apparitions, specters and ghouls and phantoms, standing sentry along the path inside the cavern. They were the critters that hid and taunted me when I was traversing through the corridor and appeared as shadows fading in and out through the walls and some slithering like Serpents. They gave off the same vibes that chilled my blood to the very bone soon after being captured by the ship, perhaps captured and abducted by them and brought into the ship.

At the light at the end of the tunnel inside that specter-infested cavern a human looking man and woman, both standing up straight and at attention or so it seemed, and apparently waiting for me to arrive. I didn't notice if either of them had a stopwatch and were timing me during my journey through the maze that they had funneled me through, and then my bizarre trek to reach them in the final stretch. They came up to me and extended their hands, both the man and the woman at the same time, and I shook their hands, the woman's first, then they stepped back (robotically) to the position they were in when I first entered the room inside the cave.

No furniture, tables, chairs, couches, sofas, computers, televisions, or bears, were in that part of the cave other than the mechanical man, woman and me. They looked human and communicated verbally with me once I was in the room/cave with them. I saw no recording devices, note pads, pens or pencils, smart phones or any gadgets whatsoever, and no stopwatches. They were dressed professionally and displayed a cordial and pleasant demeanor towards me. All the other critters in the cave just outside of that room kept their distance and remained peaceful and quiet in the background.

The man spoke first and asked me if I had any questions so far about the ship? I nearly gagged and choked before exploding in hysterical laughter, and then after regaining my composure, I said, "a few." I couldn't be angry, annoyed, exasperated or frozen with fear, or even very inquisitive, since I was still breathing the happy air or whatever it was that was keeping me mellowed out, serene, joyful and slap-happy goofy.

I asked them, "isn't prolonged giddiness, pleasure and non-stop joy, mixed in with pure insanity, terror, and the epitome of bizarre, dangerous for the mind, body, and soul after a certain point? 'Too much of a good thing can't be a good thing, my mom once told me.' And I told them. "Mom never said much about too much of bad or crazy things and what they might do to a person's mind." On Earth, I couldn't hold on to giddiness very long and wasn't sure I wanted to; and certainly, not under perverted situations as thrown at me in this ship. Not that I could ever recall being giddy at a funeral over a dead goldfish; happy sometimes, yes, with the arrival of a new goldfish for my aquarium.

People tend to frown on overly lightheaded people who are stuck in dire situations and remain happy, believing them simple-minded and perhaps candidates for the funny farm." I said to the man and the woman (authoritative figures in my mind at that juncture). I sounded a little exasperated as my mind wavered back and forth and then seemed to have reverted to my childhood mode, as I spoke with them.

I unintentionally blurted out "that spending all this time on the ship thus far primed me for the insane asylum." I wasn't sure what reality was anymore. And I asked, "how long have I been on this funny farm of a ship?" and "where are you guys taking the other people and me?" And "what gives you the right to snatch, kidnap people from their homes?" I rattled off a least another hundred or so questions that had piled up in my mind up to that point in time. I wasn't sure I made any sense or that I was anywhere near coherent, being that the dang-blasted giddiness that I could not shake loose, diminished much of the edge in that one-sided conversation, when one is trying their darnedest to be taken seriously and not look the fool.

I failed and looked the fool, and I was foremost confused in mind and spirit during the time I stood there in front of the toy-soldier Aliens in human dress and drab; blabbering incessantly and incoherently to them like a mixed-up child attempting to look and sound intelligent. During my overwrought agitation, I would have peed my pants, but I didn't have to go. Which raised additional questions, "why didn't I have to use the bathroom the whole time I was on the ship?" I asked. "Which could be months per my amateur calculations?" I said. "Was that a direct consequence of being on a ship where time was absent?" I timidly inquired.

They let me spew my nonsense and unintelligible ramblings for a considerable length of time and to the point where most of my questions became increasingly jumbled and far too tangled for them to attempt to untangle even if they were supreme beings. They avoided answering my juvenile questions. Then, the man told me that some of the disclosure of what the ship was about, was forthcoming.

The woman then spoke, "we are taking you and 999 of your fellow humans, total of a thousand (999 plus you) to a planet (star) located in a far-off system that is perplexingly different from your planet Earth and star system. You and the others have been taken out of your human bodies and given an illusion of being inside of your human forms. When the preparation for the first leg of this journey completes, the ship will divide (split) into two ships, one with the human bodies inside the preservation tubes and one with the soul essence of the humans on this ship (you and the other humans).

The ship with the souls will continue at a great rate of speed towards the star you will henceforth forever exist on (should you choose to do so), and the other ship with the physical bodies will remain in the solar (star) system that we have removed your bodies and souls from. No explanation for the reasons for the preservations of your bodies is forthcoming to you or any of the others on this ship. All of you will receive new bodies soon after your arrival at the star of your destination. The bodies you will receive will not be human-type bodies, but spirit forms suitable to your new lifestyle and environment of your choosing. The ship split apart some time ago, and the human portions of you and the others are now in distant orbit around the star of your planet in its furthest reaches, on the very edge of the star system we picked you up from."

Unconcerned about the news of my old human body, I spoke up and enthusiastically blurted out, "I'm fervently looking forward to this amazing cosmic journey. I was never truly happy on Earth and struggled to find peace in my life and believed that I had found it during my semi-seclusion away from the big city and living close to nature. But I didn't, I was miserable being alone and craved to rejoin my family in the town I grew up in, but had no desire to admit defeat and crawl back to them. Is that why I and the others got picked for this planet transfer program?" Because we couldn't find lasting happiness on Earth?"

The woman laughed and said no, "other more pertinent reasons and circumstances that concern the type of soul of your origination, is why. Everyone on this ship, when placed on Earth, had special human bodies provided to them that differed considerably in DNA from other humans on planet Earth. DNA and blood types are similar for each of you that are on this ship."

"You were placed on Earth for purposeful and meaningful reasons that related to DNA that is both physical and ethereal based. Most humans only have the physical aspect of the genes that make up their physical bodies, and minds, and the mystical, spiritual elements are missing, turned off or toned down considerably for most normal humans."

The man said, "You and the others will go through programs that will prepare you for a new reality on your new planet (star). A reality that resided inside of you from the onset of your existence. A reality which was subdued and placed on hold while you, unknowingly, assisted human physiology and technological progression on planet Earth. Some of you held academic degrees, but none of you received accolades for the work you have unknowingly or knowingly done. You, and the others on the ship, covertly and secretly passed on to humans, knowledge and biological material while working and existing around those who benefitted, also unknowingly, simply from and by your presence in their lives, regardless of how little that presence, occurrence, and dealings with other humans, was."

Somehow, deep inside of me, I knew I was not fully human, I was something else, and now that I know that, I have a chance to live the life I would enjoy living, for eternity. Enjoyment not just by chance or the spirit of the

94

occasion or seasons, holidays and so-called special days such as birthdays, that happen on Earth. For me, those days seemed more of a drain on my energy and any potential enthusiasm I might have had, had I not been on Earth. I never understood why true happiness eluded me. Now I'm happy all the time and will be happy forever; nothing can keep me from it. I asked them, "am I happy because I'm out of my human body or is there something in the air in this ship that keeps me giddy?"

The man in the room told me to "continue exploring the ship and that I would find that answer for myself, and eventually the many other unanswered questions and mysteries of the universe as well." After saying that, he and the woman vanished from the room, like magicians performing a disappearing act on a stage. For me, it was Christmas with all its presents and all the other holidays I treasured as a young boy, all rolled up into one. All that human magic lost its meaning for me during my teenage years, and I stopped celebrating and enjoying the holidays, which seemed pointless fabrications to me. Friends and family continued celebrating without me, and I moved my focus towards more practical and constructive activities. I didn't fit in with human affairs and beliefs, and now I understood why.

I loved my human family dearly and now struggled with the idea of leaving them behind, perhaps forever. I just wasn't one of them and could never be one of them, full humans as they were. Cosmically, we were different souls and on far different eternal paths traveling through the evermore mysterious universe. We were not birds of a feather even though we shared some of the same genes and characteristics. That thought made me sad, and tears dropped from my illusory nonexistent eyes. I knew then, at that moment, that our paths would never meet again. The woman chimed in telepathically, and said, "not necessarily, you can choose to see and be with them and even help them from a distance or much closer if you so desire. They will not have the same options or privileges as you have, and they can't contact you. And if you help them they will not know it was from you, and will likely credit it to good fortune or chance." I was happy to hear that I could, at the very least, help them!

I simply disappeared from my family; my body was alive on a ship that was permanently set adrift in the vastness of space and marooned around my old star system and allowed to drift presumably forever in the abyss of dark space. For what reason or purpose, I wasn't to know at this stage of my awakening.

My family would be devastated, not knowing what happened to me and they wouldn't have my body to entomb in the ground of Earth, and put me and their anguish to rest. It wasn't my nature to up and totally disappear. So, they would suspect foul play, believing perhaps I had been murdered by someone and my body left in some farmer's field to rot, and my bones dragged off and eaten by wild animals. There was nothing I could do; I couldn't send them a message and by the time I received my full powers at some future junction, much time would have passed on Earth. Much time had already passed on the ship (none at all according to what I heard at the pool), still, something passed, processes happened and will continue to happen until the ship reaches its destination. I learned I was on the ship six months and had three months more before the completion of my instructions. Six months if not a whole lot more, had gone by on Earth but not a single minute on the ship elapsed. Soon, I would be living on my new planet and undergo my continual ascension process.

EROPMANOP

The little information told me by the man, and the woman, had my mind swimming in glorious expectation. Even though I didn't have a physical head or body for the mind to operate from, as they said it was an illusion, it all felt tangible and real to me. The illusion was real enough, and I felt whole and physical as I did before I found myself on this ship, and more so. I decided to look for the pool of liquid-wisdom and deep knowledge and sit in the mysterious solution and breathe in the vapor of enlightenment that radiated illumination from the water of life. The maze that was my life was a complex structure that I would add to and build on for the rest of my stay inside the confines of this universe.

I lost most of the baggage and delusions systematically embedded inside my soul while on Earth as a human during my strange dance in the labyrinth inside the ship. While searching "through" the hidden meanings and mysteries that I believed belonged to and concerned the ship, were in reality about me and my life. The ship stripped me down to my bare bone of a soul and left me naked of my past.

I found the pool of water easily this time without searching for it through the maze of rooms. I removed my nonexistent clothing and piled them up with my watch on the side of the pool. I still had my wallet filled with credit cards, driver's license and some cash in it, and my iPhone that I kept in the pocket of my jeans. My leather belt, my trusty running shoes (sneakers) that I wore until they fell apart and I bought new ones. My blue jeans, the same thing, wore them until they came apart at the seams, that was what made up the bulk of my wardrobe back on Earth, and my button-down shirts. All in a pile that looked and felt very real to me.

I floated on the water which was amazingly comfortable, and let my mind wander and absorb the sensations of infinity.

I quickly learned that my soul type was sanctioned and excluded from the reincarnation process and the barbaric and stringent karmic regiment that many human souls were destined to endure. That the suffering through recurrent cycles of death and birth, routinely was the edict placed on humanity, existing across the galactic spectrum on numerous star systems and their planetary hordes.

I learned that my parents and siblings had to suffer through such human ordeals too, and my disappearance was one such ordeal they would have to come to terms with, that I was dead and would never return or be seen again by them. The fact that my body would never surface would be a long and arduous road for them to journey. I learned that death and separation from loved ones were part of the despair levied on all humans born with the karmic gene.

My soul-mind increased exponentially during my extensive absorption of material straight off the cosmic waterways, which I floated on and that held on to me like an umbilical cord attached to the ship and directly into my mind and soul. My whole being glowed like a firefly in a dark, mysterious forest as I metaphorically drank from the waters of the pool. The others on the ship with me, my compatriots, were growing and glowing at advanced rates in other parts of the ship in their unique amniotic pools as was I. We never saw each other and never communicated openly (face to face) during the consolidation of information period.

The focus was on our individual development alone, and distractions found no fertile ground in any of our souls during that time. Our minds were connected temporarily, and we were aware of our group progress without the casual chit-chat or other mental impediments.

The man and the woman who met with me privately also met with each of the thousand members privately. The man and the woman occasionally interjected material into the group mind. It was never a question and answer session at this stage of our learning process; only pure information released for us to indulge and absorb directly into our individual minds. I learned that the learning process began the moment I set foot on the ship. Because all of us boarded the ship at different, timed intervals, we absorbed information that corresponded to each person's moment of arrival and need. Not everyone picked up by the ship carried the same amounts of distracting baggage and were picked up later. I was not the first to be picked up but belonged to the group that required more sludge removal than the groups of people picked up last.

Moments after entering the ship, the ship instantly stripped away my flesh and blood body from my soul and stored it in the glass jar and into one of the Frankenstein laboratories. I was made to forget that assault on my body with all the distractions from the strange critters and fantastic scenery inside and outside of the craft. The critters created my illusions and added and removed things from my mind-soul while on a metaphorical conveyor belt stripping me of my mortal human identity and juxtaposing a new reality on my soul while keeping remnants of my old reality until the process was complete.

We, the no-longer-humans on the ship, reached a point where we could individually disconnect completely from the group-mind and even from receiving personal telepathic messages from the man and the woman, our direct contacts while on the ship. We could go on our own and do whatever suited us most to do or learn, independently. I, as was true with the others, was already a fully autonomous being even before reaching Eropmanop. Ego-driven souls, we were not; we simply possessed immense latitude of freedoms that are unknown and out of reach to the physically-endowed lifeforms that make up a large percentage of the biological mass of the universe.

I became aware of most everything about the star we were heading towards before we reached Eropmanop, as did the rest of the crew. The star remained a distance away from the ship, but it already existed inside our individual minds. Eropmanop is a star that could hold millions of Earth-size planets within it, as was true with the star that Earth revolves around that is called the Sun. But Eropmanop was not a typical star as Earth's star is, far from it. Eropmanop is a star that gives off no light and remains hidden in the night sky.

When the ship made its approach to Eropmanop, thousands of similar ships made their approach to Eropmanop. The alien ships identical to our ship harvested beings such as ourselves from other planetary star systems across the galaxy. Harvesting hybrid humans was an ongoing and endless process inside most galaxies. We, the newly harvested, were to join forces with others on Eropmanop, who were making their way to other parts of the galactic kingdom for fun, pleasure, diplomatic tasks, and any number of personal and collective objectives and desires they wished to be involved. Some members of Eropmanop would return to the star after venturing away. Most from Eropmanop would never return to Eropmanop, losing themselves in the matters most important to them as they traveled anywhere and everywhere in the grand universe including leaving this universe temporarily or permanently in search of other more intense realities and ventures.

How each soul traveled was up to them alone. I could, after I graduated from Eropmanop, craft ships to fit unique situations for personal demands and needs that suited travel requirements of my choosing. The mind-soul we possessed could transit through space without ships or other physical and nonphysical apparatus. I could craft and create ships and soul containers after or before reaching chosen destinations when and if there was a need for such equipment as physical or ephemeral devices.

Eropmanop is a bizarre dark star that didn't shine like other stars in the Milky Way galaxy. Eropmanop contained information, physical (physics of another order, a much broader order) and ethereal, a mystical material important to us and our future endeavors inside of the cosmos. To initialize (become whole) we had to go to Eropmanop and be galvanized and initiated by pairing our souls with the star (become one with the star). There was no requirement on the length of our stay on Eropmanop, and we could leave after a short immersion into the Star. Some members choose to remain on Eropmanop their whole existence, never leaving the star, others as myself, departed soon after confirmation.

I learned why I was sent to Earth and placed into a hybrid human body. A body that protected me from many earth elements that would have otherwise jeopardized my mission on Earth, by damaging me or killing my physical body. I didn't know it until now, how much of a shield my hybrid body provided me while on Earth. Earth is a messed-up place that I knew from living on that planet for thirty-six years. That's why I came to Earth, to get a feel of humanity and what it was like being human. My real mission was multifaceted and mostly biological in nature, where my interactions with the people I met were crafted and directed by fellow beings from Eropmanop without my awareness and knowledge. My human body contained genetic material and acted as a living storage unit for multiple people in my vicinity, who received from it microbes, viruses, bacteria, and pathogens, placed into other humans by my Alien compatriots.

I was directed to move to my house in the boondocks by them, the Aliens from Eropmanop and they placed me in contact with all the people who, in my mind, came into my life by accident or coincidence (I never suspected otherwise). My sexual encounters with human women were engineered also, and every encounter with a female produced a fetus inside the woman I had sexual intercourse with, even when I used protection. The women never suspected they became pregnant in my short interludes with them (one-night stands). The resulting fetuses were removed in the early stages (a few days) after conception, during ensuing abductions and placed into other human women on Earth or taken to the ship for storage. Some fetuses were placed with other types of humanoids on other planets and moons. I was only one of thousands participating in those types of programs across the planet incognito in numerous covert operations by Aliens, who sometimes worked in conjunction with some governments. But most things Aliens do on planets like Earth remain hidden from humans forever.

I didn't need to suffer many of the trials most non-hybrid humans had to suffer during their lives on Earth. I became aware of the daily hardships and dramas that many people faced and endured until death. And death only being a temporary and often short delay from the spirit tormenters, for some of Earth's wayward inhabitants.

I had no information on my parents, siblings, and friends concerning their lives and situations on Earth. I didn't have any of the details of their past lives and why they were doing time on Earth, other than they were doing time on Earth. To know more intimate details about them or others on that planet called Earth required that I return to Earth after I fully arose and fused into my future life's joyful work.

Unlike full humans or other types of human hybrids, there were many sorts of hybrids of my caliber and soul species. I was new to the muddled version of consciousness on low levels of existence and the so-called "reality" in the highly illusionary and delusional-prone Earth-type societies therein. This stratum of dimensions, where chasing one's tail (ego) is considered progress and encouraged by cultures which exist to distract its member citizens away from what is right, is beyond my level of comprehension and understanding, but I hoped to grasp some of the meaning of it as my knowledge base increased and expanded.

My total experience of the physical and mortal world comes from my short tour on Earth (or so I believed at that early point of my awakening). The rest of my awareness manifests while on this ship. We on the ship are embryos, tethered to the ship's innards and growing inside a membrane where our souls and minds feed while traveling through space until the moment of our breach, whereupon the mothership will birth us onto the star, Eropmanop.

Soon after the ship's arrival, the ship inserted itself into Eropmanop, and like a spawning fish, released us into a cavity whose walls, ceilings and floor were covered with jagged, crystalized mineral formations. It was a place not suited for walking or traversing by physical beings of any type; the star repelled physical beings. My arms and legs were missing, and my torso hovered about the ship inside of an embryonic pod holding my soul within it. Each pod with a soul was later injected individually into unique and private cavities deep inside of Eropmanop; in one of the millions of large caverns existing inside the star. We emerged from the ship spiritually nearly intact, crystallized with layers of knowledge attained while voyaging inside the ship. The rest of our heritage, we would acquire through spirit-melding with Eropmanop.

Eropmanop had a dense surface and porous strata under the surface that made up a large portion of the star. The core of Eropmanop was hollow and consisted of massive structures in the shape of pillars jutting out from the center to all points of the porous membrane that surrounded the core. The outer shell of Eropmanop was rough and jagged and looked like a spiny fruit or seed pod.

Streets, buildings, vehicles and other forms of transportation for the masses, didn't exist on the star. Shopping malls, grocery stores, farmer's markets were absent and unneeded. Entertainment venues, such as theaters, musical bands, orchestras, sports stadiums and the like, existed nowhere on Eropmanop. Zoos, farms, animals, plants and insects had no place on Eropmanop, except for digitized or replicas of such things, stored in personal compartments, crevices, caverns, grottos, rooms, caves, and so forth, by beings as me.

Water, oceans, seas, rivers, streams, lakes, aquifers or even a water cooler to drink from, could not be found on Eropmanop. Eropmanop was as dry as cotton. No ice on the surface or below the surface. No snow rain, sleet or any kinds of moisture existed on the star; no storms, clouds or weather phenomena of any sort menaced the Eropmanop star.

I missed the water, having been privileged to enjoy water sports, ski slopes, hot chocolate, and ice-cold beer during my short life on Earth. I could indulge my memories and only regretted that I hadn't taken the advantage to create more enjoyable memories while I had the chance on Earth. However, now that I'm much more aware I would not trade places and become human again (so I thought). I now exist in a persistent pleasurable state of mind, where the whole universe is my personal playground. My body, mind, and spirit are forever pain-free and incorruptible. I need no food, drink or any stimulants whatsoever and will exist for eternity in my present but ever growing and expanding reality of my sole making and choosing.

I lacked the primal physical need for companionship as what was preeminent on Earth. On Earth, humans could not be whole if they were by themselves, alone, without a partner or spouse. Which was a sorrowful ache that plagued me the whole time I was human, more so than any other human discomforts I experienced on Earth.

My human compatriots who did time on Earth with me, came from similar backgrounds as did I. We didn't make permanent attachments as getting married and having children would have entailed. We were programmed that way by those who knew and understood the workings of human psychological and physical needs. We lived modest and secluded lives and often watched life go by from the sidelines, as associates and friends shot past us with their careers and families. Painful it was for me, and I assumed for all of us, who were stuck in the purgatory of Earth while unknowingly waiting to be rescued by our kindred from Eropmanop.

Not that we were being punished for past life discrepancies and having to do a short stint on Earth for redemption purposes, since we had no debaucheries to account for, having had no previous physical lives to create such missteps and baggage. We were truly just off the turnip truck (so I thought, and now know otherwise), green and uncooked in the pressure cooker of multiple previous lives as most humans are, well-seasoned in the reincarnation games, even though most humans don't know it or show it.

Eropmanop is a fascinating star with many mysteries embedded into it, not only for the occupants such as myself, but within the endless nooks, crannies, and fissures inside the star. Each of us occupied a niche, a grotto, chamber or cave and there were endless billions of niches and grottos and such inside the massive and infinite labyrinths and mazes incorporated in and on the star, Eropmanop. Niches provide a place, a sanctuary, not only for our souls but for our individual collections of things that some of us will spend eternity amassing; for our personal pleasure and, indirectly, for the benefit of the whole universe to peruse through, for information concerning our cosmic sector.

Like honey bees, souls from Eropmanop travel to and fro in this galaxy's star systems, collecting the nectar of information and material objects and adding them to their assemblages inside their nooks and crannies. We don't take without giving something in return and often tenfold in return for everything we take or borrow. Equipped with the knowledge, the power and the keys to the universe, we bequeath generously and accommodatingly, all we have back to the galactic progeny deserving of it or in need of it.

Now that I and my cohorts are fully matured, having been christened by the star Eropmanop, we can travel and amass as much or as little as we wish, or nothing at all. None of us need ever return to Eropmanop if we had no desire to do so. Nevertheless, our grottos were ours forever to do as we wished. Those spirit souls that didn't return to Eropmanop, nevertheless had a place that was uniquely theirs for eternity.

A group of us Eropmanop agents chose to materialize into corporal bodies, and invaded certain planetary terrains that were in early stages of humanoid development in new star systems. We teamed up and visited planets as tribes and lived nearby the natives of the planet and traded goods and ideas with the native peoples. The natives, the children of earlier creations by the local gods and overlords, assumed we were simply another tribe in the area that they would ultimately have to compete with and eventually war against. Tribe leaders sized us up, to determine our strengths and weaknesses soon after we made ourselves known to them. If weak, they attacked and swiftly conquered, killing the males and taking the rest as slaves (non-human surrogates we planted). When the new tribe was stronger, they plotted and bided their time, while outwardly showing friendship.

Most of the contrived encounters with the natives were peaceful for a period until they determined the level of danger of the newcomers (us). Sometimes, tribes took no chances and attacked our tribe soon after our presence was detected. We could destroy the tribe or leave the tribe alone, and simply vanish back to the stars or relocate to other parts of the planet and engage in other encounters with other natives. We have done all the above during our many excursions in the physical realms of newly inhabited planets, as well as varying other stages of advancement, up to and including, space-age societies.

For chosen tribes, tribes of people we had an interest in helping to succeed, due to the fact they showed promise and ingenuity, we were the gods that came down with space machines and dwelled among them, the primitive people, as chiefs, shaman, and priests. We imparted advanced knowledge and gave them unique abilities that allowed them advantages over other lesser and barbaric tribes of people.

We of Eropmanop, are nation-builders and nation destroyers, often in conflict with other gods and other beings who have come down from the stars with their peculiar designs, motives, and objectives, concerning planets and the populations of people on the planets. Battles regularly ensued between tribes and then nations, both on the ground and in the air. It was a means, a strategy to force tribes of people into innovating while taking out the trash (the rebel extraterrestrials infesting the area). Tribes that failed to innovate failed on their own and fell to the wayside and went extinct on their own. Some tribes assimilated into larger tribes voluntarily or by force of the stronger tribe members. Smaller tribes naturally fell to enslavement by the stronger tribes in the area as a perverse equilibrium and raw natural order of human nature, that often evolved with our help.

We watched and documented endless thousands of such human/humanoid ordeals play out under various situations, climates and threat levels, without much interference from higher beings such as us. However, we, and many other higher beings, did stir and add to the evolutionary pot, frequently.

In the galaxy, exist numerous Eropmanop stars with their unique motives, strategies, missions or whatever the masters of each star wished to do and be. Occasionally, such emissaries from the stars had clashing ideologies, duties or objectives that boiled over into skirmishes and sometimes battles. Mostly, such battles were between rebel clans of beings from various star systems, who were looking to expand their races and cultural biases across other planetary systems where they were unwelcomed guests.

Beings such as myself, often clashed on a planet while nurturing projects and people that have fallen into conflict with any number of Galactic Alien beings. There are numerous galactic rogues that shun galactic protocol and become involved on planets and moons throughout the galaxy, unsolicited. Some are intentionally harmful beings, others, like those from Eropmanop stars, are intentionally benevolent beings. And between the two resides a slew of other types of temperamental and outright belligerent and aggressive beings.

114

I chose to work alone most of the time, and many of my caliber of entities, also did. I showed up on a planet and explored its unique traits, features, plant, insect, and animal life and documented everything that interested or fascinated me. Other similar beings, are the Johnny Apple Seeds of the cosmos, who seed and bring unique varieties of flora and fauna and nurture such creations for as long as they deemed necessary. Beings as myself from Eropmanop stars, mostly collect things and share knowledge with indigenous lifeforms, intelligent or not. We infuse and manipulate (mutate) genes of all living things we encounter in our travels across planetary systems and leave our distinct mark on DNA strands throughout the sector of the universe allocated or adopted by us.

Seldom do we make ourselves known to the races of beings we meet, influence or terminate. Contact with any race or species can be as short as microseconds, minutes or last hours if not days, weeks, months, years, decades and even millennia. Every action we take is documented and forever stored on Eropmanop stars, for the use of other beings.

Each of the planets and the moons have their unique time slot determined by rotation around the star, if it is a planet, and rotation around the planet if it is the moon. We view time for what it is, a malleable tool to use for whatever purpose we individually, but sometimes collectively, deem fit. We come, we go, without any thought of time, schedules, calendars, watches, or the rotations of planets and moons. We don't look to the stars for directions and can never lose our bearings as we trek through the cosmos, in whatever means we choose, and that best fits the occasion.

Duplicity is not what we practice or do (most of the time). Everything above board is our guiding procedure, principle, and protocol. We catalog changes on planets, moons, comets, and stars too, and anything else that has an effect on life, intelligent or otherwise. We do what we do because it's enjoyment, fun and entertaining for us. We don't work, and we don't work for anyone or thing, we volunteer and participate when it suits us; we relish what we do and do what we relish. Nothing is monotonous for us, and we look for every detail and make a note of it from our unique point of view and file it in personal files and store it along with memorabilia, for eternity or thereabouts.

As is true of honey, made by bees for themselves and their colonies, there is honey aplenty for non-bees, like humans, bears, etc., who want or crave honey and are searching for honey, for themselves to enjoy or squander. The bees that created and make honey have little say or control over their honey. Same with us Eropmanop spirit beings, we amass information that becomes available for the taking by those who had no hand in creating it. Our personal files and extensive collections of everything imaginable, are readily available to anyone in need or want of the information we collect and organize. For those who have the means or have approved access, are free to obtain and harvest from our massive storehouse of invaluable information, stashed away into unique individual hoards.

Eropmanop is a cosmic library, archive, museum, and depository of all types of information and gadgets discovered in this small sector of the universe, which consists of dozens of galaxies and billions of star systems. There are numerous types of storage facilities far more wide-ranging and complex than Eropmanop stars, in every galactic sector. The universal mind is the big kahuna when it comes to cosmic information, and administered by other beings than we of Eropmanop. Eropmanop planets only provide a small taste, a feeder, that makes up only a fraction of the massive trove of data available in the cosmos.

We don't take physical evidence, material from planets, moons, stars, comets or the billions of rocks flying endlessly through space. We take information, and if we deem it essential, we will recreate and replicate exact copies of any item we consider interesting, and place said items inside niches on Eropmanop. Information stored on Eropmanop stars emanates and radiates freely throughout the sector/quadrant of the cosmos that is served and is picked up and accessed via paranormal channels by multiple types of beings.

MORTAL PROBLEMS

Earth is one of many planets with mortal problems. Mortals, who, for the most part, are oblivious to cosmic reality and easily manipulated by other mortals and the multitudes of invisible cosmic paranormal beings that come and go as often as the cold virus. Mortals, enticed into making decisions by beings from Eropmanop and other cosmic paranormal beings and creatures invited to the party by the actions of each mortal, is a common affair in the physical realms. Mortal minds are constantly bombarded with ideas to influence them to make the leap in one direction or other. Mortals, slow to make decisions (procrastinate), will have decisions made for them by any number of beings that happen to be in the area at any given moment in time. Depending on the individual's soul value, decisions made for them can have negative or positive consequences; with long term or short term effects that the mortal will have to deal with during their trudge through life.

When I happened to be in any particular area or region for whatever reason during my endless travels, and I become aware of a mental blockage a person is experiencing, I can intervene on behalf of the person. I might whisper into the person's ear ideas to help smooth their constipated minds into making a decision. Fifty percent of the time my advice goes in one ear and out the other, as is true with most great advice, regardless of where it comes from or originates. When that happens, I simply move on to other things of interest to me without a second thought, knowing that indecision is natural and one of the quandaries afflicting human minds. Other beings and creatures, some with ulterior motives, might spend far more time in their attempts to mislead or enlighten a person, especially if the person is in a weak state of mind brought on by stimulants or personal negative actions that weaken human minds and souls. Depressed and evil minds, are easy prey for ravenous beings lurking and searching for amusement and opportunities to torment vulnerable humans.

Humans exist to be tested, and tested they will be, from birth until death. Death separates people briefly from the madness of all the testing on physical realms. Every day of a person's life is a test of one sort or other. And all types of beings, scoundrels and benevolent, love adding ill will or good will into the mix; both negative and positive. Negative beings are not held accountable for their actions and disruptions on human souls, and positive beings receive no rewards for their sage advice when helping human souls. Rewards and consequences (if there be any), go to those who act out the things that originated in their minds or deposited into their thoughts by spirits and made into realities by the receiving person/soul.

I have seen humans ganged up on by negative beings who pound them with negative thoughts mercilessly and are allowed to do so by the higher beings. My positive interjection of valuable information, should I choose to give during such assaults, has little chance of entering due to the incessant abuse by negative beings. I can alert positive beings to rush in and sometimes do, but most of the time, the positive spirits already know and have abandoned that soul (human) to the negative beings. That usually happens after a long and futile fight by the positive beings that produced little or no fruit worth saving.

A downward spiral brings on a feeding frenzy that attracts additional negative humans and negative spirits into the fray, like sharks to spilled blood. At such levels of desperation, positive spirit beings and human ones too, throw up their hands and leave the train-wreck to be cleaned up by the creatures and the maggots of the underworld. Such humans often have lived hateful lives and brought or caused, untold misery to people around them and in turn face the consequences of their own making.

The upswing for people in the positive trajectory and moving upwards is pleasant to behold, but also a precarious ride; that can draw in negative spirits and humans who wish to derail, upset the apple cart, when it gets near the finish line. I marvel at the human spirits able to throw off daily assaults and hold their own without losing their focus to do the right thing, always.

I had an easy life in comparison to most humans during my short time on Earth as a half-human. Nonetheless, I fully appreciate the trickery and constant battles most humans face while on Earth. I was protected and shielded from the negative powers, whereas most humans are fair game to negative wretched forces. I would add, unfair game, being I'm fully aware of the crafty and shrewd beings that peoples' souls are up against. In some situations, it's a David and Goliath struggle of good versus evil.

It's amazing the number of characters, good, bad and indifferent that exist and thrive in the spirit and physical realms. Sometimes, and some places, it was thick with beings doing their dances and trances around the human and other such critter-elements in the animal world. In many places, countries on Earth, the stewpot was kept on a constant boil to extract the deep-rooted evil from the souls, through the relentless hardship of mind, body, and soul.

As a spirit among spirits, we from Eropmanop, were aware of each other but seldom communicated with each other unless, or until, we joined forces on some specific operation. It's a whole different experience in the spirit world compared to the physical world where humans coexist, argue, laugh, horse around, tell each other jokes and fight over miscues and misunderstandings. Communication between humans can be a minefield and a hazard for those humans not born with a diplomatic gene but saddled with a big mouth instead. Nevertheless, most conversations between people trend towards cordial, more so when they are among strangers.

The conversation between spirit beings from Eropmanop had little purpose and mostly a distraction away from things that matter to them individually. Spirit beings aren't handicapped with ego, envy, hate, greed or a need for a hug, when things got the better of them. Nothing gets spirit beings down, unless they were spirits from the other side of the tracks and mean-spirited. Spirit beings cared nothing about sports, the weather, politics, health issues, climate change or the endless gossip and the incessant dance of human drama for the sake of drama, and therefore, had nothing to talk about with each other. Spirit beings are emissaries for other higher up spirit entities, and more than not, indifferent to the chores they are assigned to do, or chose to do on their own, for any number of reasons, as is true for me and others from the stars.

I came to Earth often as a free agent and documented many of the things that had fascinated me back when I was a human on planet Earth. Not much of what is on Earth fascinates me now, having seen so many truly captivating cosmic places, planets, moons, and stars. However, as a child and while growing up on Earth, I was easily charmed by some things, whether they be extraordinary or not. It was my personal memories that I wished to preserve and keep in perpetuity inside of my niche. Unlike humans, whose memories and every second of their existence gets recorded for them, by beings such as myself and others, I had to record my individual stuff and therefore was equipped with a proficient memory at birth for use during my short time on Earth.

Because I haven't had to die before switching realities, my memories remained intact with me without disruption, inside my mind-spirit from day one of my birth on Earth. Such memories are momentous and forever a part of what I am and will become during my existence in this and many other universes that I will progress through.

Each personal grotto on Eropmanop could hold enough material to fill a planet the size of Earth a hundred times over if not a thousand times over. I haven't even begun my explorations of the cosmos, only having explored a few dozen planets and a handful of different eras and time zones; and twice as many moons, stars, and other space debris thus far. Space debris was a potent cosmic soup made up of shards and rocks that once belonged to planets, moons, and star-material that was originally spewed and cast off the surface and innards of the sun.

During my visit to Earth I learned all there was to know about my immediate family, my father, mother, brother and sister and their growing families (my nephews and nieces), who had grown in number by three, two nieces and one nephew, since the time I gained freedom from Earth. I fulfilled many of their wishes and desires during my incognito visit with them; those I could ethically fulfill for them, and a few that I snuck in. And I planted many positive ideas into their minds and watched a few of those ideas come to fruition. I will continue to nurture them and many others on Earth only because I can. I do enjoy seeing my family, their friends, and other humans unrelated to my family prosper with a little nudge from me.

In my perpetual gladness and joy, it was nevertheless painful to look back on some of the lives my family experienced, that brought them to where they are now. Nothing evil, but many mistakes and misgivings that held them back from becoming more than they did, during

125

the courses of their previous lives; situations that created more problems for them that they now had to deal with and resolve in their current lives. I was hoping I could shorten their reincarnation cycles, and learned that I couldn't, unless other situations by them could be realized and met by their free will choices. Loopholes existed in the cosmic order that I'm not free to disclose in their entirety in this document.

I am part of the angelic Corps of beings, which are a group of spirit beings whose souls are markedly different than human souls. The caste, race of spirit beings that I belong to, parallels, in degrees, with the pure spirit beings who have never been subjected to living in the flesh. Such pure beings serve multiple strata of realities, which encompass many layers of spirit and physical domains. Karmic beings are part of the angelic forces known as the Pure Ones.

Pure beings are extremely private beings and divulge scant information about themselves and their mode of operations. Whenever I cross paths with such beings, I attempt to extract information from them, irrespective of their unwillingness to divulge. That's what I and others in my line do, extract minute information and details from everything and every situation we encounter, regardless of the difficulties and dangers placed on our very souls and existence. We take notes and diligently study all things inside and out, to the very base and depth of desolation.

Angelic beings possess a highly-sophisticated type of soul whose ranks seldom get breached by other spirit beings of lesser caliber. Unlike other souls in the soul arena, angelic souls have existed forever, as they are without progression, as many soul types require. Their numbers increase and decrease, as cosmic sign waves, determined by elements in their vicinity, and eternally exist everywhere their domain is, and their domain is everywhere they are.

Angelic beings are machine-like in nature when they enter the lower and inferior realms of their domains. They don't communicate verbally or telepathically; they release information methodically and briefly by entrenching into the mind, whatever they wish to convey to whoever it is they wish to convey. I approached one such being and instantly understood what it chose to disclose to me. It was like a pre-recorded standardized message. The spirit lacked detectable emotions that I could capture and store into my stash of information. Had I been human, it would have responded differently towards me, since such an encounter necessitated a dissimilar setting than where my present spirit strata resided. I was not privy to what a human encounter with such an entity entailed, being that

each encounter is unique and germane to each person
encountered.

COSMIC RIFFRAFF

Eropmanop was much more than a sponge, sopping up material and information from around the galaxy and beyond; it also had a more profound bent and purpose. The star and its many sister stars, acted as monitors, detecting and regulating conditions inside the galactic sectors where they presided. Eropmanop stars functioned like Endocrine Glands that regulate hormones in a human body. I, and others like me, were the hormones, alerted and released, whenever situations arose that needed instantaneous attention and further monitoring in any number of star systems in the galaxies in the quadrant.

We brought balance and determined the cause of disruption to the relative order of the sector monitored by our presence. Whenever a breach from enormous waves of undesirables crossed into the quadrant in numbers unsustainable for absorption into the available new star systems, Eropmanop deployed countermeasures for deflection. Such incursions received immediate lethal responses that neutralized the greater portion of the invaders. Those that managed to survive and penetrated system barriers were tracked down and dealt with individually. The portions allowed to live and to hide out, and who eventually got pressed into service by overlords and other rulers charged with managing star systems, tended to flourish rapidly, like cancer after taking root.

That inclination of the Eropmanop stars carried with it eternal ramifications for inscrutable systems behind many of the types of beings associated with the segmented parts of galactic quadrants. Quadrants that consisted of billions of star systems allocated with certain privileges denied to other sectors and quadrants inside of galactic control. Some quadrants acted as sanctioned breeding grounds for multiples of negative beings of the types that infested and infected low realm planets such as Earth planets. Planets where my kind of spirit beings embedded, due to the richness and wealth of material primed for harvesting on a regular and rotational basis due to the infestations.

Activities by multi-ethnic, pluralistic and diverse beings attracted to the earth realms are monitored and recorded ardently by my compatriots and I. Information gathered appeared in a communal mind-zone, as the means of knowledge pooled to avoid duplicity and to alert others of possible conflict or potential impending hardship. On many occasions, I have tracked down and documented the activities of wayward creatures that flashed across the cosmic regions like ocean waves against the rocks. Not for exposing them, for them and their purpose is well known and often sanctioned by the gods, and even sought after by numerous cosmic hierarchies and organizations. I pursued the practice to satisfy my curiosity and sense of duty, and by doing so, I provided the inhabitants of the quadrant unbiased snapshots of activities, surveillance, and pixels of the life inside this dimensional zone as do all like-minded spirits along with assistance on many levels from Eropmanop.

In one such instance, I tracked a rogue clan of beings that managed to make it through galactic defenses put in place over a moon belonging to a planet that had a hundred-plus moons orbiting it. The star system that the planetary system belonged to was a typical system in the quadrant. The quadrant harbored many thousands of similar yellow stars that averaged fifty orbiting planets in various sizes and their hundreds of moons and thousands of moonlets.

The moon in question was well developed technologically and had several vacation spots and cities under individual domes on the surface of that moon. Inhabitants (humans mostly) of two of the blue planets in that star system had populated several sections of the star system's inner circle of planets extensively and created many recreational and commercial retreats on numerous moons. Six planets of various sizes made up the inner planets, and the outer planets numbered more than forty and in various sizes. Half were large planets and most had Saturnian rings; the rest of the planets were smaller and shrouded in clouds of meteors, space dust asteroids, and comets.

On the moon of my study, the population consisted of human-type beings, whose lifespans were past the century mark, around a hundred years or more. They had maladies similar to Earth humans and common to these types of star systems and planets in the quadrant; maladies that were far less severe and minimal in comparison to those infecting Earth humans.

The Reptilian beings I observed were one in a class of thousands of similar races and species of beings that contaminated and populated portions of the galaxy. Like worms, this race of Reptilians quickly penetrated the moon's surface with their ship and lodged themselves inside one of the abundant natural caverns beneath the moon's crust. They then proceeded to build out their hidden lair before going dormant for a time and did not emerge for several weeks while they molted in place. The duration of shedding (molting) varied, depending on the race of Reptilians. After being covered with layers of the material that flaked off the Reptilian skin the cave was ready to receive live humans and human corpses.

The Reptilians were aware of me but could do nothing to keep me from observing them. I could have alerted the overlords in charge of that district if it weren't for the fact the overlords already knew about the infestation on that one moon and sanctioned this merry band of thieves and their covert operations. Nevertheless, I was only obliged to make reports to Eropmanop and not to the local overlords and other authorities of that planetary system. Most of the time my presence was unknown to all including the highest powers-that-be, the rulers, gods and other spirit beings within the spectrum of realities and covert powers incorporated in that star system.

It was seldom advantageous for us to alert any of the local authorities about anything we were doing or involved in, due to the component that it, made our presence in any area and time, "known" and that, compromised our mission. Our work was best accomplished in complete obscurity to the local gods and overlords, whenever possible. We are untouchable and beyond the reach of most entities, gods, and beings in existence because we are members of a higher order of spirit entities.

As officers belonging to the order of the Eropmanop empire, it was our duty (always voluntary) to work through proper channels that operated mostly behind the scenes of planetary management systems and hierarchies and the puppets on strings with the appearance of running things. Planetary gods and overlords were not the true rulers but only acted and performed their duties within a range of protocols and directives set in place by the higher order of spirit super-beings. Beings that we, of the Eropmanop order, worked directly with and sometimes through them and for them.

Once the Reptilians emerged from their lair, they began abducting humans from the domed cities and resort areas, where people flocked to vacation spots from the inner planets. The Reptilians took the abducted down into their cave and removed biological material from the women, men, and children. Material that had been placed "into" them when they were young broods by the same Reptilians or by others such as the Serpents. Serpent beings previously abducted some of those people and inserted into them various bacteria that would grow and mature at an approximate and timely rate; usually in the span of twenty earth years. The Serpent biomass, often confused as tumors and cyst by the humanoid doctors, was harvested by Reptilians at the behest of the Serpents.

Sometimes the Reptilians abducted married couples even when only one of the people was the carrier of the Serpent material. There was an element inside the Serpent material that spread between the copulating couple that was reaped and harvested, and used by the Reptilians for their "own" purposes. Abducted single people carried a more potent microbe in their bodies that didn't dilute when they had sex with numerous other people. The Alien microbes understood and avoided multiple partner situations and shut down (went dormant) when contact between partners wasn't biologically consistent. Nevertheless, Reptilians would track down and contact all

135

the one-night-stands and remove any residual bacteria that originated from a Serpent encounter.

Mutations due to human biological tampering by the Reptilians, occasionally created plagues that destroyed whole towns and cities throughout the ages and on many planetary systems. Some such situations were intentional and allowed to happen or made to happen to remove identified humanoid races that carried strains detrimental to human populations in the region. Humans infected were exterminated, isolated (quarantined) or both. We of Eropmanop were on a constant lookout for signs of outbreaks of any kind and origin that didn't get to the stage of manifestation. Had I stumbled onto something that was imminent I took steps to stop it or contain it. At which point, those in charge of the area took it from there.

Reptilians in human form met with Serpent-tampered people at gatherings and at beach parties where they knew their targets would be. Most of the domed cities had beaches and many kinds of water sports where single people met, congregated, and partied into the night and the day, often for a week or two at a time during their vacation periods.

The Reptilians shapeshifted, and their appearance became like one of the crowds of people they infiltrated inside the domes. Reptilians didn't always use drugs to capture humans when the meeting was casual and away from the party goers and alone in secluded spots for romance/sex. Though, Reptilians facilitated (used) common drugs that were locally available, including alcoholic drinks to subdue their human prey.

I observed two Reptilians in human costume approach two women in a bar, had a few drinks with them and then asked them to dance. After a few dances, they led the two girls off the packed dance floor, literally put them over their shoulders and carried the kicking and struggling women out of the building. No one took notice or made attempts to stop the two human-looking men (Reptilians) from kidnapping the two women. Most everyone in the bar was intoxicated and oblivious to things going on around them or didn't want or cared to get involved. The Reptilians took the two young women outside the building and placed them into a stealth vehicle and vanished down into the underground nest. The girls were intoxicated after a few drinks at the bar and unaware of what was happening to them but did put up a futile struggle. Reptilians are powerful and can easily incapacitate a human male or female without the use of drugs. Reptilians used various drugs on some humans for reasons of memory distortion and amnesia for humans they planned to release back into the human population.

Inside the cave, the two Reptilians reverted to their Reptilian form and injected the women with a tranquilizing venom administered from a hidden claw that sprang out of one or more of the Reptilian fingers. Having been sedated by the Reptilians, the women's bodies then were spun into cocoons by the secretions released from the limbs of the two Reptilians. The process was like a spider wrapping a captured insect onto its web. The two women then were stored inside burrows hollowed out previously to hold cocooned humans.

In the place of the two women, androids or clones took their place and their demise from an accident or medical trauma used in the coroner report, soon followed. Other times the people simply disappeared and treated as runaways unless or until bodies were recovered by the local authorities.

Not all abducted humans were immediately or swiftly taken down to the caves underneath the moon's surface as those two women were. Sometimes the humans were taken to hotel rooms near the beaches, where the Reptilians had sexual intercourse with the unsuspecting humans, who believed they were dating other humans. It was not always clear why some humans were taken for a longer duration into the cave, and some were only taken to rooms to copulate with the Reptilians and then released to return to their planets of origin unharmed and biologically untampered.

Reptilians, even those employed by the overlords, wished for most of their activities to remain elusive and often crafted false scenarios strictly for appearances, for the gods and overlords, who seldom and infrequently checked in on the Reptilians and their doings. All humans contacted by Reptilians got tampered with biologically and on the spirit level to some degree. Attempting to decipher the reason or purpose was near impossible due to every situation, and each human tampering was exclusive to each person tampered with.

At first, it wasn't always clear to me if the Reptilians did it for sexual pleasure alone; they didn't tranquilize the humans during the encounters, only partied with them on a one-night-stand basis. For longer periods, if the Reptilians desired to prolong the encounter for whatever reasons or until the human had to return to work on their home planets and were no longer required or useful to the Reptilians.

Sometimes the abducted people, during dreams, would see bits of their nightmarish affairs with otherworldly beings such as the Reptilians but never make connections to what the dreams meant or suspect they were real encounters in real places on and off their planets of birth.

I followed one of the human women who returned to her planet after having spent a week "dating" one of the Reptilians and mated several times during that week. Female humans didn't use contraceptives but could, with simple, nonintrusive devices, know if they had conceived, almost immediately; and could keep or end the pregnancy with those same instruments without the need for doctors or anyone knowing about it, not that anybody on that planet cared.

Pregnancy or termination of pregnancy was a non-issue on that planetary structure as it was on all the planets in that star region. There was no required wedlock, and many humans chose not to have children or wed. But just as many people chose to have children, which balanced things out. Much of the workforce was automated and robotic, and that allowed more freedom to the human inhabitants to indulge many types of leisure activities. However, most humans had jobs to perform in many diverse fields and industries of their choosing and abilities.

Soon after the woman returned to her home on her planet the young woman waved a device over her abdomen to check on her condition, and it turned out negative, she was not pregnant. That made me curious about what the purpose was for the Reptilian having sex with her. Reptilians never miss and usually impregnated females with their first encounter, if that were their intention and mission. The extended meet with that woman by the Reptilian, turned out to be for other reasons besides impregnation. Reptilians had human contact for a plethora of biological harvesting and implanting and using humans as long term and short term incubators. I did a further exam on her, without her knowledge and found nothing, no implants, residues or other tracking devices on her body. The Reptilians knew I was watching them, so they maneuvered their activities to keep me guessing about their motives and schemes.

I couldn't be in more than one place at a time and was handicapped against such cleverly deceptive creatures as the Reptilians were. I could recruit others of my breed to join me, but my psychic communications were vulnerable to interception by the wily and cunning Reptilians. I had the ability to create and launch additional Pi devices (personal androids), but that too would only trigger countermeasures and other complications, diversions, and strategies by the Reptilians, who managed to subterfuge my schemes with their opposing schemes. Clever and incredibly deceptive and crafty, was why the gods, overlords, and others in the cosmic realms employed Reptilians for any number of covert projects.

I went back to the cave and observed further the Reptilian clandestine activities. I noticed cocoons that hadn't been there the last time I was there and witnessed the two women placed into cocoons. The cocoons were large containers that held things the size of humans but also smaller ones for animals, pets, cats and dogs and other types of animals. All the cocoons fit snugly into shafts burrowed into the solid rock inside of the cave made to fit each cocoon. The humans on this planetary system were the same size as humans back on earth, five feet tall on average for the women and six feet tall on average for the men. I inspected the new cocoons and noted that people occupied the cocoons, the very people that the Reptilians partied with and hung out with on the surface of the moon. I then noticed that the girl I had followed back to her planet was inside one of the cocoons. The Reptilian had taken the girl's form and identity and returned to the planet posing as her. The Reptilian posturing as her and checking her abdomen for pregnancy was a ploy to throw me off the trail.

The complex situation created by the Reptilians, who were masters of spinning mind-twisting webs of their covert activities, required long stretches of persistence to document, and I normally relinquished lengthy and complicated labyrinth-type projects as this one turned out to be. Following such ordeals consumes a lot of effort and rarely produces comprehensive conclusions of what is "really" going on. The universe brims with dead-end diversions by powerful beings who have the power of maneuvering space and time to their advantages, for the purpose of skewing reality and usable and traceable information.

I was helpless to assist that girl as I was the other women entangled in the Reptilian web. Whatever it was that put them into the situations they were in, had to play out. The gods allowed it, and I didn't know if the gods were not behind the whole thing from the start. The gods knew I was there due to my extended activities and could detect all of what I was aware of, doing and pursuing. I didn't cloak all my material and my activities, which goes against protocol on the lower planets that I sometimes attempt to comply. Taking on or killing Reptilians in the service of the gods and overlords was against planetary decorum and I abided most of the time. Random extermination of undesirables who posed threats to humans and humanoids was in my rights and obligations to perform. However, these Reptilians had sanctions, and therefore, I could only monitor their activities or move on and go about my business elsewhere. I chose to monitor the situation further simply for my records.

The cocooned girl lost her identity to a Reptilian who took over her persona and occupation on her planet. Such persona-switching happened and happens and are not unique incidences; other Reptilians had captured and replaced humans in that planetary system and other planetary systems, and continue to do so. It is not a literal body switch (not always), the Reptilians mimic the person and assume the roles of the human by morphing their Reptilian bodies to resemble the human victim. The morphing was not precise but good enough that even close friends and work associates could not tell the difference. And those who could see a change always assumed it was in the realm of normal. Humans tend to modify their appearances with makeup, hair color, hair cut or style or dress in different attire and clothing. People age quickly during duress, constant travel, a switch in diet, deteriorating health issues, and any number of things they encounter that affects them, their temperament, their physiques, and how they look. Therefore, those things and other life altering situations, played into Reptilian schemes and dealings with humans.

I followed the Reptilian who had taken up the life of the woman. The Reptilian was annoyed that I hadn't moved on and tried to ignore me as it continued impersonating the woman it replaced. She worked in the travel industry and visited many of the company-owned resorts located throughout the star system. She frequently traveled to the company's resorts and stayed a week at a time, sampling and enjoying the activities offered at each resort location. She would then do a report on her experience at the vacation spot and turn it over to her supervisors. That's how her company kept tabs on their far-flung properties and resorts, by using incognito employees such as her to perform the monitoring. The staff was aware of surprise inspections done by the owners but didn't suspect her. The Reptilian that took her place could do her job as well as she, if not better, having stolen her memories directly from her mind before dispatching her and cocooning her body for storage in the cave.

The woman's job and her position with the company, were ideal for obtaining access to numerous places in the inner planets and moons, while remaining incognito and under the radar. Reptilians were building the groundwork and the network to infiltrate and become an integral part of this solar system and the humans in it. I recorded many types of Reptilian species that had established themselves on various other planets inside of that solar system, mostly residing on two planets on the edge of the star system. Reptilians were aggressive in their intentions to infiltrate the inner planets, specifically two of the planets that were nearest the sun of that star system.

The girl was dead, and her soul released to journey yet again to reincarnate into another child, in the belly of a woman, her new mother, on the same planet that she originated before being captured by the Reptilians and killed by them. She reincarnated without the short interval between lives as some human souls receive when they die with a minimum of decorum. Her body was preserved inside the cocoon by the Reptilians for additional biological materials that they'll harvest for a time before disposing of the cadaver at some later date. Frequently, Reptilians will keep biological material from certain humans indefinitely and therefore, keep the cocooned bodies of those individuals preserved underground on moons, planets and cargo ships drifting in space.

Not all the humans cocooned were dead, some were placed into hibernation or a coma and kept alive for extended periods for further biological manipulation and harvesting by the Reptilians. Their souls hovered outside their bodies for a time, and some souls departed immediately after death or after being placed in a coma, and their souls moved to the higher cosmic grounds to await their outcomes. Such souls had gotten released from their bodies by higher spirits in charge of their souls. All the people in the cocoons would die or be killed, eventually, by their captors, the Reptilians, and their bodies put into unspecified storage inside caves on that planet for future processing.

Most of the humans on those planets weren't subjected to Reptilian tampering, only about one percent of the population fell into Reptilian webs, and fewer still, lost their lives from those encounters. One percent from every economic stratum of the human population on that planet was the norm for Reptilian harvesting. That star system didn't have a diverse human population as Earth has. This star system had a population that was homogenized early in its development into one race of humans and lacked racial discrepancies and differences as found on Earth. The humans on that planet experienced economic disparities to a far lesser degree than on Earth. I closed and recorded my findings in that Reptilian case and carried on with other interests.

My alcove (niche) on Eropmanop burgeons with information I have gathered from planets, moons, stars and inhabitants of the places I have visited. A helper I named Pi, of my creation and designed specifically for my interests and desires, accompanied me wherever I went. Pi scanned and digitized items and materials of interest to me and sent the information instantly and directly to my alcove on Eropmanop. Solid items Pi regenerated as exact replicas (copies) of the original items and the information cataloged and stored on Eropmanop.

On a whim, I entered a hummingbird to experience being a hummingbird on one of the planets belonging to one of the stars in the galaxy. My experiences were collected and documented by Pi while hovering at my side. The exhilaration of rapid "physical" flight, the sights, and sounds and the taste of nectar from the flowers and the occasional skirmishes with other hummingbirds over mating territory, were recorded from my perspective. The hummingbird's perspective was already known and documented by the creators of hummingbirds and stored on other systems in the halls of cosmic information. My experiences were only documented by me and stored into my personal collection for perusal by others in some future, past or present era.

That same planet, which was void of humans and other semi-intelligent creatures, was populated only with gentle creatures, magnificent forests, babbling brooks, rivers, and streams. I experienced many other varieties of birds, animals and aquatic life while Pi documented every succulent moment for me. The planet had its type of uniqueness, where neither carnivores nor herbivores existed. Animals on the planet mated and populated without the need for consumption of food, as is necessary for planets of Earth status. Birds didn't eat insects and insects didn't eat other insects. It was food and poop-free planet, as are many millions of such planets in the galaxy. Everything had a lifespan of months for some and years for others. At the end of a lifespan, animals and insects dissolve into the atmosphere instantaneously. Nutrients for growth and sustenance was in the air and taken in through the lungs. Biology on a far different order than what exists on Earth and other planets, thrived on these types of planets.

That planet, only one of many types of spirit wonderlands and amusement parks on planetary scales, where spirits could immerse their souls into many types of animal and insect creatures. Both in the macro and quantum regions with physical aspects, without the physical trauma of existing only to find food and quench momentarily, the insatiable curse of craving food that many animals on regular planets suffer through. Nor did the creatures and those who would inhabit them, need to fear being stalked, captured and eaten by predators. For the morbid spirits in need of such thrills, morose planets existed, primarily for the perverse lower base desires of the interstellar bottom feeders.

TIME SPHERES

I had all the time in the cosmos at my fingertips to do whatever pleased me to do. Time exists only inside time spheres of designated space delegated by and for the pleasure of higher powers in the spirit kingdoms. Invisible "time spheres", to humans and other beings and creatures existing in the physical universe, who are unaware of such realities. The spheres are not invisible to me and those in my situation (Spirit class).

Time spheres existed everywhere in the universe and encapsulated zones of stars (hundreds, thousands, millions, etc.) and their planetary assemblages. Smaller time spheres held one or a few stars and their planetary systems within their grasp. Quantum microscopic time spheres appropriated time sequences of atoms and their manic sub-particles. Many sizes and types of time spheres exist in the vastness of the universe of which the full purpose of the phenomenon I had yet to extrapolate, experience and explore. It is far too huge a task even to contemplate but a fraction of the marvels in existence and little need, due to the infinite numbers of beings that continually document most everything that happens. Only the portion I experienced concerning the time singularity at any moment, entered my hoard of information on Eropmanop, via Pi.

"Time cubes", as the author of this book named the segregation of time phenomena in earlier writings, is a misnomer. Time is not only cubed spaces of time but mostly spherical, like bubbles and balloons. Bubbles that easily burst and balloons that can expand and become larger or shrink, contract and become smaller. What a time cube or bubble is, depends on what the higher spirit beings want the time manipulation to be, which changes over "time" by design of those beings with the wherewithal to make changes to cosmic time and space. Time confinements are fashioned into any shape, form, and size and generally are globular and spherical.

As I delved deeper into situations about time-sphere-dimensions or anything else I endeavored into, the new information filled in the missing blanks instantly and automatically, without further input or awareness of the process by me. Pi managed all the tedious details of my endless and ever-evolving intergalactic itinerary and projects.

Significant amounts of information existed inside of time-spheres that are warehoused deep into the hollows of quantum space and could be extracted and used by spirit beings wherever in the universe they might be. The coded information is chiseled out and brought to life, for the use by designated humans ordained to uncover aspects of Alien biological technology, chronologically or as needed.

Inside a time-sphere, time calculates and manifests by the time set on the time-sphere by the administrators of said time-spheres. That chosen time standard henceforth applied to the time on each planet and their moons and was not determined or calculated by planetary rotation around a star. Some star systems continued to use planetary revolutions around stars as the official source for time keeping.

Time was most irrelevant to the gods and the overlords of the star systems, who used time sequences as one of the adjustable tools for controlling segments of the cosmos. Overlords and gods, by the virtue and decree of the superior spirit beings, were allowed to remain out of the confluence of time while administering subordinate beings under the rule of time. Time is most relevant to the inferior, subsidiary populations of various races and classes of beings that used commerce and trade between planetary systems to keep track of economies governing populations in the physical realities.

Dimensional time-spheres were manipulated and placed in arrangements and conglomerations by the super-beings for any reason that suited particularly crafted situations for planetary administration, such as what types of creatures made up the inhabitants of a star system. Massively large creatures, far greater in size than the largest dinosaurs found on Earth, required time disparities to fit gravitational proportions on massive planets. Such, being only one of any number of qualifiers for warping and shaping time-spheres to fit the essential occasions designed by the overlords. Time and space mimic and exaggerate distances and movements of stars and galaxies, confounding humans on most planets in their attempts to understand the universe and its origin. The universe has no origin, existing always without expansion or contraction.

Time-spheres can be any size and cover small areas of space and thereby create confusion and act as shields against unwanted rebel forces and others not allowed in restricted districts around or near planets, moons, space cities and large spacecraft in the human zones. Time is a reusable commodity with finite adjustable boundaries using infinite malleable properties. Time is not a constant it is a controllable quantum element and a paradigm and a dilemma for the physically impaired (flesh and blood humans and humanoids) trapped inside the web of time.

Spirit beings exist simultaneously in a state of macro relativity and in the subatomic quantum of timeless space, where the only true freedom in "this" universe, resides.

I entered a different time-sphere from the one I resided in, and altered I was for an instant in my mind and soul. Like the light spectrum with its shades of magnetic waves, time hides mystical anomalies between the strands of dimensions it displaces. Space and time within a time-sphere differed substantially from one time-sphere to another and exaggerated the spirit and physical rhythms of those going from one to the other, as when transcending and leaping from dimension to dimension.

I was captivated by the mind-altering effects inside the time spheres, however acute they were for lesser, corporeal beings. Properties that didn't affect me, or apply to me in my spirit form did apply to physical forms in curious ways. Those effects are part of the mind-confusion that snares mortal minds in webs of illusions in the three-dimensional mind-zones existing in all galaxies. Similar properties occur inside paranormal craft (UFOs) used by entities who have constant and regular dealings with humans and their ongoing soul projects.

I moved through time periods between decades and millennia with the ease of traversing a light spectrum, but with the occasional diminished or amplified spirit abilities. Not all time-spheres performed the same, and some properties inside of them are more stable than others with numinous (mystical) manifestations that are disorienting, like running into oneself in both spirit and bodily form at the same time while remaining separate and detached. Extremely annoying and distracting for humans caught momentarily phasing in and out of their physical bodies while taken and given rides by extraterrestrials inside of Alien ships (UFOs).

No fixed parameters to the time spheres exist, if it's not a large vortex of time. One can find themselves outside of the time-sphere, with a challenging, disoriented mind, and find themselves lost in time, space and dimensions. A hazard for physical beings and some spirit beings, whether they be inside a spaceship (UFO) or accompanied by higher or lower spirit-beings outside of an Alien ship during an abduction of the soul and traversing through space. Situations that can arise when out of a corporal body, as in remote-viewing situations and other such out-of-body spirit phenomena.

Out-of-body souls are always accompanied by higher spirit beings, who remain, for the most part, incognito (hidden) and out of sight and mind of the soul that has been yanked free from their body temporarily by the spirit being. Out of body never happens on its own, as is believed by many who have experienced leaving their bodies. Often trusting (erroneously) that they created the situation themselves via intense meditation.

I could venture into the Roman era of two thousand years past and feast on Roman cuisine and take in a show at the Coliseum while sipping and nipping on morsels of time. And an instant later, be on a modern-era cruise ship eating dessert and savoring the bites of manipulated time pastries. Transportation of people and things from one era to another happened under various guidelines, but a practice in violation of treaties on some planets and star systems. People, animals, insects, and plants were moved around from place to place from one planet to another on different timelines by planetary maintenance engineers.

Histories and time zones exist at the same time, unlike the ideas of time travel which are false in the literal sense, because real time exists not and everything is on the same linear space. The cosmos consists of every conceivable period on various planets in the galaxy and within planetary systems at any given time (all the time). On Earth, we have modern space-age countries existing next to medieval countries, where living standards haven't changed for thousands of years, and people are living in huts and drinking polluted water, next to people drinking clean water and living in ultramodern skyscrapers. The same is true within galactic star systems sporting numerous planets and moons that harbor scores of flora and fauna from various time zones.

Diversity within planets and moons is massive and out of the sight and awareness of human types of peoples. Including humanoids, who lack the human genes and other far more mysterious types of beings existing side by side with humans as well as living on the surface of planets and moons, and in the vast incomprehensibly massive innards within planets and moons.

In many star systems with multiple planetary conglomerations made up of dozens of planets, are many levels of historical diversity. Planets as near to each other as Mars and Earth, where one planet is pre-space-age and the other planet pre-human-age, with monstrous animals like dinosaurs, roam and rule. On other planets, civilizations are ancient and exist in constant battles between warring barbarians. Others exist in a Renaissance-type era or any number of eras, including space age people who are fully aware of the diversity of their star system. People from advanced planets know to not tamper with the less-advanced people but sometimes, under strict etiquette and rules, are allowed to visit or even vacation among the backward people while remaining disguised as the natives or hidden from them via cloaking of ships and habitats.

DABBLING IN THE FLESH

Greek stories and the Greco history piqued my interest as a student in high school back on Earth. That, and other whys and wherefores, I decided to experience the life of an aristocratic Greek citizen before the era and the rise of the Roman Empire. I plotted a romantic tryst with a young elegant Grecian woman who captured my admiration when I was last in her village on a mission from Eropmanop. Long after the mission completed, I remained in touch with her without her knowing it, and I viewed her from the spirit world where I observed her growing up and blossoming into a beautiful woman. I became a Greek not through the birth canal of a mortal Greek mother as I could have chosen to do to coincide with her birth and grow up together. Instead, I stepped into the picture and into the role of a Greek aristocrat, straight from the spirit world and into the physical world where she resided through a dimensional door of my creation. After materializing into a physical human body of a wealthy Greek merchant, I traveled to her village in a caravan also of my creation. What I didn't fashion or make I bought from local merchants and markets. I procured my needs with replicas of coins Pi minted for me. I also bartered for goods, food, wine, horses, and laborers as my needs arose to fulfill my whimsical enterprise.

The lovely woman I set my mind on enraptured me with her grace and simple charms. She belonged to one of the leaders of the village who was born into wealth and had managed to hold on to it thus far. She was well educated, energetic, and the epitome of a Greek goddess, though she was not a goddess. She possessed the attributes I was interested in to fulfill one of my many fantasies of living the life of an ancient Greek noble. It was a situation that unfolded naturally without much finagling from me and with latitude for a quick engagement and then marriage. She was unlike many of the aristocratic women of that town and era, down to earth in her mannerisms and possessed a pure and good soul. She was naturally attractive, and I was handsome (by design), and we immediately clicked and fell for each other. The attraction and magic were real as was the romance. Traditions, customs, rituals, and sheep trading, I had met, and I preceded without a flaw to the bridal chamber with her and consummated the marriage.

I fulfilled my husbandly obligations of the marriage agreement, all the while I took the time to become part of the community. I built for my bride and I a prestigious villa that overlooked the Aegean Sea from where we would raise a family. We lived a long and blissful prosperous life together until she aged and passed away. I then met up with her on the other side where we continued our open relationship to this day and endlessly in various other life situations that have blossomed since.

Such scenarios are common practices on these levels of reality, which are infringed upon and created by spirit beings of every stripe and origin since forever. Physical gods (rulers) also indulged in such brazen practices routinely, as a means of injecting their offspring into populations that they shepherd and cultivate in the open as the gods who came down to Earth to assist the spread of humankind around the many lands in need of habitation. Gods have intensely interacted with humans overtly in ancient situations, and just as surely, but covertly most other times, present and future.

I avoided the normal quarrels, haggles and drama of traditional marriages by the abundant use of wisdom enhanced with the magic of diplomatic persuasion. My Greek wife produced four children for me over the course of seven years (a blink of an eye considering I had done so many other things during that mere slice of time). My children (offspring) carried my genes and my type of soul, and are therefore hybrid humans who exist without the reincarnation genetic factor that encumbers souls stuck in the physical abyss.

My Greek family knew not who I was and believed me to be a typical wealthy Greek man, who traveled by land and by sea; and unbeknownst to them, by air to other parts of the world and worlds, as a means of making a living so as to keep my family living in luxury. I provided for my wife and children and spent time with them on several occasions as they grew and matured. I took them on amazing adventures off planet (unbeknownst to them) and to vacation spots and trips to other lands on the planet of their birth, by the illusion of caravan and by ship (UFO). I protected them from diseases, illnesses, and plagues that afflicted others in their village. I spoiled them no less than others in that time-era spoiled their families in the aristocratic arena of the gods and treated them far better than the typical human Greeks of similar standing.

My wife was fully human, and my children were like me when I was human, hybrid humans, and they, in turn, would become members of Eropmanop and have their compartment, niche, cave, to fill with their delights and desires when the time came. My immediate family didn't know much about my cosmic origination and superhuman abilities, but they suspected I was not part of the human breed as was most everyone else that they had contact with in the village, including the extended family members. They believed me an eccentric foreigner from a strange land.

I continued to travel into past times, present times and future times and spread my seed far and wide as it suited me. I was a devoted father and husband (when I married) more so than most human married men could ever dream of or claim. I had advantages in every endeavor I pursued and therefore the luxury to provide well for my offspring and their caregivers, my spouses and concubine lovers (mistresses). Situations with no advantages I avoided, not wishing to subject the family to risky enterprises and life situations that would have brought hardships to them. It was my privilege, my prerogative, and duty, to do the best I could for those I brought into this world or the many other worlds. Had I done less, I would have been a monster and a failure as a father and immortal spirit being. There are no shortages of monsters and failures who despoil their offspring, spouses and create living hells for them and other family members, friends and associates because of who they are, degenerate souls.

I was not a martyr, masochist or degenerate and had no intentions of living a life of drama or engage in battles to prove my bravery (ego). For me, such human ideals were foolish and depraved since I didn't need to engage them during those episodes of family life on physical planets. My family endeavors and designs were for pleasure and propagation of my seed and less about documentation, for the sole purpose of raw information for files on Eropmanop, which they became, nonetheless.

Yet, on some occasions, I have chosen to soldier in the physical realms and go on campaigns as a means of documenting the experience for my archives and not for vanity or heroics. Most full humans had no choice in such matters as war during their lives and did so for the pure reasons of the survival of themselves, families, villages, and nations. Situations (wars) often contrived by higher beings who shifted the sands of time and space for the benefit or the punishment or both for their cosmic underlings put through such horrors and trials.

Creating and dishing out hardships presented as destiny by the controlling and tampering gods, is what gods do on these lower levels of existence. I had a choice most of the time when I occupied a human body on what I would encounter and be compelled to deal with. But nothing is one hundred percent, when playing in the physical realms on planetary systems impregnated with ingeniously devious spirits and beings who ply their trade for pure evil and treachery, and occasionally for the long term good, for the vilest and the sweetest of souls and reasons.

CAPTURED

A Serpent Android captured me during one of my corporal escapades inside a human body on a planet similar to Earth. The Serpent Android took me to a large ship above the planet and stored me in a section of the ship with other humans that it had collected (captured) earlier. I protested profusely explaining to my Android captor that I was a spirit being and thus exempt from seizures and tampering by beings as itself while I ventured in physical enclaves. I had protections and guarantees against flagrant abductions and meddling in my affairs by the likes of it, the Android. The Android spoke to me and said I had no such exemptions while inside a human body during that "specific" era inside of a time-sphere. And without another word from the Android, I was shipped off with the other human herd to some distant planet in the star system within that peculiar time-sphere, with its own unpredictable and ambiguous physical and spirit laws of governing.

The Android bound my wrists as if I were a captured slave, my new reality in captivity. I lost most of my powers that I had as a spirit being and now subjected to whatever whims and degradation the Serpents had in store for me, and the other humans snared that day with me. I didn't know where I was and where the scum was taking us so brusquely, as the victims of these pirates on nightly raids on helpless villagers. I was not fearful believing that I would somehow figure out a way to outmaneuver and outsmart the villains that had imprisoned me inside the maze of the astrophysical time sphere I placed myself.

I'd become used to absolute autonomy and couldn't imagine losing it so easily to an inferior robot and its masters. The Androids tied us up as a precaution to protect their human plunder because some of the humans on the ship were in a rage and lashed out at other humans in the cage with them and were damaging them. Having been captured and corralled like wild animals, the men kicked and screamed like wild donkeys and trapped hyenas. Despair and confusion were apparent in the screams and yelling by the men caged with me. Friend or foe could not be distinguished in the dark shadows inside the cages and fights broke out between the herded humans in their desperate attempts to escape the unknown hijackers; until in turn, they were all tied up by the Androids.

The drones culled the meek, weak and damaged from the strong and belligerent and placed them in separate cages. Women were taken to another section of the ship and separated from the men. The damaged were killed and disposed like garbage. Blood covered parts of the cage floor, and splattered blood dripped from the bars from the occupants. Disgusting odor and stench from the sweat and fear from the brawls hung in the thick and musty cold air. The raunchy scene and the cruel episodes of savagery that unfolded between men and men and machine (Androids), epitomized for me the perils and insanity of living amongst mortal men driven to beasts.

Trapped inside a physical body, I remained calm and passive knowing that there had to be a way to escape my unexpected deplorable predicament and I continued to search for opportunities to escape the madness. Because of the type of being I am, I took advantage of my mishap and documented in my mind one of the endless facets of the bizarre and sickening situations frequently sprung on humans as they trudge through life's gruesome quirks in various times and places. My awkward and unforeseen experience forever recorded in my head, my mind, since my sidekick Pi was confiscated by the Serpent rustler drones that captured and subdued me.

Clustered and categorized by the Androids who used mysterious metrics to segregate the men into six groups, the Androids removed us from the cages and then loaded us into shipping containers. I belonged to the largest group consisting of two dozen men, the less violent and restrained bunch originally stuffed into the cages like

167

sardines with the men that had gone crazy mad. The powerful Androids picked us up with their massive hands and carried two men at a time (one on each hand) into the containers. Each segregated group had their containers and a little more elbow room but not much. The drones closed the doors and sealed us inside the pitch-dark metal boxes the size of a tractor trailer. Soon after the Androids closed the container doors, a liquid mist drizzled down from the ceiling of the container and covered us with a sticky, slimy residue. The tranquilizing mist knocked out most of the men, and they fell quickly asleep. A few of the men moaned and groaned before acquiescing to the drugs in the mist. I was drowsy but remained awake longer than I wished I had. The drones left us hogtied and bounded inside the containers.

At our destination, wherever that destination was, the container door opened. There was no way of knowing how long we were inside the metal box. The drones cut off our bonds, and we limped along and made our way to another section of the ship where feeding tubes protruding from the ceiling awaited us. Ravaged and parched from the long trip and near starvation, we instinctively latched on to the dangling tits and sucked profusely like ravenous calves on the udders of a cow. The substance from the tubes was a thick and rancid tasting liquid, and within moments of feeding on the tubes, we regained our strength.

Amnesia affected most everyone after consuming the disgusting gruel from the dangling tubes. That and from the mist that draped over us the whole time we were inside the containers. I remembered what happened to me, but I noticed that the other men were oblivious of their past lives, the lives they had before being abducted and stuffed into the containers by the Androids. Talking amongst the men was minimal and akin to grunts. The terror in the eyes of the men before being placed into the containers was now gone. The men looked calm, drugged and lost inside their minds; some walked and some hobbled around timidly looking at the walls in the room with blank stares.

We lingered for a while before the Androids came back and began taking men four at a time to some other place on the ship. The group of men that had gone berserk with fear and kicked and screamed the loudest before being hogtied were not with our group. They were separated from us and placed into different containers that were taken to some other location somewhere on the ship.

During our drawn-out stint in that place, we continued to feed on the tubes, the only source of food and drink available to us. At some point, several days I guesstimated, the taste and consistency of the material from the feeding tubes changed abruptly and drastically and became more appetizing. Soon after, I noticed slight variations to my physical human body, which I attributed to the change in diet.

Our quarters had beds on both sides of the aisle, and the place reminded me of a military barracks from when I was in the army back on Earth. Not long after we arrived and fed like herded animals, the Androids stripped us of our clothing and left us naked. Nude with no gowns to wear, nor shoes or slippers for our feet we existed as common slaves. The building was comfortable concerning the temperature, neither hot nor cold. We had sheets on the beds but no pillows or blankets. The building or ship had no windows and no way to see the outside of the structure and no way to distinguish between day and night. A horn blast alerted us when to go to bed, and another horn blast woke us up. No clocks on the walls and no means of judging time other than the horn blasts and the dropping of the food tubes. When the rubber tits dropped from the ceiling, we knew it was time to eat and eat we did for after a few minutes the tubes retracted into the ceiling and no more food or drink until they came down again several hours later (my guesstimate). Tits dropped down four times between rising from bed, and going to bed, like clockwork, and that was my way of judging days and roughly the time. The other men didn't seem to care about time or anything else, but they instinctually raced to the feeding tubes when they dropped down not chancing missing out on the grub.

Television, radios, magazines or anything to distract our wearying minds, were not provided to us (me mostly). The Android captured me while I was visiting what is called the Dark Ages on a planet similar to Earth. I was about to set up shop and procreate with one or two of the women in the village when I was shanghaied and apprehended by one of the crafty Androids that had set up a trap for me. The humans taken with me were from different villages but from the same general area of the country and period judging by the clothing they wore and the language dialect they used. It was near the end of the Dark period, and life had improved considerably by then, but anarchy continued to plague many of the larger villages and towns.

Reptilians spread out their kidnapping schemes on various villages and various time-slots so as not to cause unnecessary alarm and panic within the villages. It was from these types of chaotic places and time periods that the Serpents reaped much of their human plunder for cosmic slave operations and breeding farms.

Body changes that I and the others were undergoing became pronounced one morning when things hardened up. I had grown another penis and now had two of them to deal with. It wasn't instantaneous; I knew something was happening down in that area of my anatomy. I noticed a nub that grew and formed over a short time and created an annoying itch. Same thing happened to all the other men in the barracks with me. The only difference between them and me was that I was aware of happenings around me and to me, where they didn't seem to notice much the developments going on in their bodies or their lives.

I was not surprised about the change in my body framework for there were, scratched and sketched on the walls of the barracks, displays of men with two dicks; graffiti by those who came through this dorm before us and had some mental capacity to make the drawings.

In the dorm, we had no communications between us; no one talked to me nor to each other, which created a dreary atmosphere for me. I existed trapped in a fog of confusion and depression that I struggled with since my capture. Androids came into the room every so often and took a few of the men with them, and the men didn't return for one or two days (judged by our wake and sleep cycles). Occasionally, the men returned the same day and looked more ragged than when taken in the morning after feeding. Some men were never seen again after being taken away by Androids.

When the penises fully formed, a few days after they became apparent, the frequency of taking men from the barracks increased. Three other men and I were the last cluster of men to be volunteered for whatever enterprises the Androids had in store for us. The same group of men at the start continued with their unknown tasks for the duration of our confinement on the ship. The Androids didn't switch us around and kept us with the same cluster of men we started out with until the end of the program.

That morning soon after feeding, Androids came and took the four of us to one of the many rooms in the building/ship. We were never allowed to leave the room on our own, and this was our first outing inside of a very large complex since brought here. The room the Android took us to was a large rectangular-shaped room roughly fifty feet wide by sixty feet deep, with soft rubbery floors and a comfortable lounging area. The room had padded walls embroidered with strange animal and humanoid designs in various sexual poses and postures. Not much color on the walls or in the room, which was mostly a bland grayish color. Light radiated down from the high ceiling and made the room sufficiently bright. Cushions, pillows and other such stuffed things of various sizes and shapes were strewn around the room.

Dispersed in the room were twelve naked human-looking women laying around on pillows or standing in various positions as if in a brothel. The female's bodies didn't appear modified or tampered with as the men's bodies had been. The Androids left the room and locked the door behind them. That was disturbing and unexpected by me. The other men with me didn't notice, but for the first time, they seem to be concerned about something sinister picked up in their extrasensory perception realms (gut feelings). Like animals, they sensed danger, as did I.

The four of us men stood there in the room near each other almost in a huddle for protection against unknown powers. Looking lost as children in an unfamiliar place and unsure what to do we did nothing but wait. The women did nothing other than lay around and took little notice of the clueless freaks with two penises in the room with them. As moments dragged on, awkwardly uncomfortable I became with the strange situation without any instructions.

Suddenly, as if on cue, all the women started acting edgy and began to fidget and paced around the room nervously. They continued to avoid the four of us men huddled in their midst near the center of the room. Then the twelve women began to panic in unison for no apparent reason that I could see. No screaming or crying but whimpering and moaning about some unseen wicked force that had yet to enter the room. The men and I didn't immediately react to the change in the atmosphere created by the moans from the women, whose rapid change from placid demeanor to blatant paranoia was swift. We continued in our huddle, suspicious that whatever it was that had the women near hysteria was about to burst into the room and ignite the party.

Like at a Roman arena, circular designs formed on the walls and then opened. Out from each hole slithered one large snake (four in all) with humanoid yet demonic grimacing faces. Not quite human but with oval heads, two eyes, holes for the nose, and a mouth that looked more human than Reptilian. Before the four of us men comprehended the situation about to unfurl, the snakes, like a flash of lightning, were up close and in our terrified faces. I nearly crapped myself when one of the snakes flew into my face as swiftly as a hummingbird but larger than anyone of us men the snake confronting me was. I could taste its rancid breath and spittle splash over my face as it hissed at me. Still huddled, we exploded in every which way to escape the four Serpents that had surrounded us. There was nowhere to run other than around the room. The room quickly became a flurry of mayhem as four naked men, and a dozen naked women scampered in every direction in dreadful unspeakable terror, chased by the four large and bizarre snakes!

The snakes murmured and taunted and provoked us as we continued to frantically try to evade the infernal beasts! The snakes were only chasing the men around the room, but the women scattered as if there were foxes loose in the henhouse, and running every which way to try and escape the inevitable. The lunacy continued for what seemed an eternity, and perspiration flowed freely from every pore of our human bodies. The room became a sauna from the body heat and the vaporized perspiration that turned toxic in a blender of madness.

The snake that was hot and heavy on my tail cornered me and stared deep into my eyes and slithered into my mind with its mind. It spoke a language that was strange, yet I understood it completely. The snake said, "catch a woman and seduce her, now!"

Exhausted from the marathon of running from the snake, I approached one of the terrified women, also exhausted, but still with energy enough to scamper frantically away from me. The same happened with the other three men who also were cornered by their own demon snake and threatened with losing their lives. Exasperated, we men stood there breathing heavily, heaving and coughing, like, "well, we tried." The snakes came at as again, and again we ran, and they cornered us once more. And the snake said to me, "catch a woman and make love to her or I will bite you filling you with venom, then swallow you whole and crap you out." And again, I chased one of the women, caught her and we feverishly copulated on the pillows strewn over the floor. Finished, she laid on the soft pillows looking exhausted and in a state of terror. I laid on the floor nearby exhausted, mostly from running from the snake and prayed that the ordeal was now over. As I rested, hoping for a break, the snake was in my face and more manic than before and demanded that I take another woman and make love to her as well.

After copulating with a third woman, I was ready and willing to die by whatever means the snake had in mind. My mind and body never encountered more brutal abuse, and my misery had become complete. At that point, I hoped that the snake would kill me and put me out of misery.

When the twelve women in the room were impregnated by the four of us men, the Serpents slithered back to their holes in the wall and said nothing more. The Androids returned and unlocked the door, and the women filed out of the room and were taken down the hall to another area of that building. We were told by one of the Androids to return to our barracks and go straight to the feeding tubes to replenish. I was starving and had an incredible thirst and ran back to the barracks with the other three men on my heels.

Subsequently, I retired to my bunk and attempted to understand how an advanced spirit as I could be captured and held by vile creatures as the Serpents. I obviously missed important information during my learning period on the ship, and now I was paying for it. I mistakenly believed myself invincible in every situation, regardless of types of dark beings that existed in these realms and this quadrant of the cosmos.

I had the ability to manifest my spirit into any physical form I wished and just as easily return to my spirit form. I had done it without complications thousands of times whenever I interacted in the physical realms. I've avoided dangerous situation while in the physical body by reverting to spirit and vanishing away from predators such as the Reptilians, Serpents, and others. But the clever Serpent Android set a snare that captured me before I could make the transfer back to the spirit and placed a lock on my soul that I could not unlock no matter what I did. The Serpent lock had two features that sealed my fate, locked me inside a human body, and a cloaking device that hid me from other spirit beings from Eropmanop, which robbed me of their assistance.

This peculiar breed of Reptilian males sported two penises, one to dispense semen to the vagina and one that inserted itself into the anus of the female and injected a hormonal fluid. The combination of the two stimulated the female to a frenzied orgasm. The intense climax induced immediate conception by accelerating the merging of sperm and egg and triggering the fertilized egg to morph into an embryo instantaneously, eliminating the need for additional sexual encounters. Reptilians are perfect and efficient baby-making machines.

The fervent orgasm produced other qualities that infused the fertilized egg and future fetus with a concentrated predisposition to a fiercely strong attachment to its mother and siblings. Reptilians are a far closer-knit family than humans.

Reptilians and humans shared a similar reproductive anatomy, and both male species could interbreed with one or two penises and impregnate both female species (human and Reptilian). In other respects, humans and Reptilians had interchangeable body parts. Reptilians have a larger, stronger muscular heart that is too powerful for the human circulatory system to withstand. Other body parts, liver, kidneys, brain, and stomach, although dissimilar were interchangeable with nearly identical qualities that functioned even with a weaker human heart or a stronger Reptilian heart. There are far more subdivisions of Reptilian races and several that have no similarities with the human anatomy.

The next day the Androids returned and collected us for another romp in the room of horrors. The three men and I that were forced to copulate with the human women the day before were taken to the same room presumably for an encore. The Androids left and locked the doors behind them as they had done the previous day. This time the room was empty, there were no human women in it. We didn't huddle, and we walked around the room or lounged on the soft furniture far more relaxed than the day before, believing that knowing what we know from yesterday's experience we were up to the task. I didn't know what the others thought if anything at all but they seemed to be more relaxed. The three men were not totally oblivious to what was happening because they understood the commands of the Androids and the Serpents that had forced their will on us the day before. Nevertheless, the men remained mostly oblivious and didn't seem to remember our previous maladies of the day before. There was no huddle, and that told me that they weren't picking up negative vibes, nor was I. Still, I wondered to myself what the Serpents had up their sleazy Reptilian sleeves this time, being that there were no women in the room to impregnate.

The four circular entrances in the wall opened, and the four of us instinctively converged from around the room and into a near huddle as the day before. A defense mechanism that failed us the previous day yet the instinct kicked in, and we merged once more. Three walls in the room had the circled outlines (four on each wall) that indicated possible twelve openings and potential horrific surprises that could overwhelm the four of us.

I knew that anything could come out of the holes in the walls from past experiences in other physical lifetimes. As was the case with Roman arenas that I had frequented for the purpose of gathering information for Eropmanop during my travels through the time spheres. Lions and tigers and other predatory beasts were often turned loose from hidden trap doors designed to catch human prisoners in the arenas off guard, to titillate the raucous blood-thirsty spectators lusting for gore. The stalking beasts in the Coliseum rushed in for the kill or took their time for a slow and playful prolonged savory carnage of the trapped human prey. Animals and humans didn't mix well in the stadium, and the resulting sickening horror and violence of beasts feeding on live humans provoked the crowds to show the level of human depravity humanity was and is. Spectators gleefully cheered, and some perverted bastards masturbated while the victims cried in horror.

Serpents didn't egress from the holes this time; female Reptilians did, four of them emerged from the openings and began to prowl around the room like wild animals. Cunning as tigers, they stalked us, the four men in the room who dreaded and feared the strange creatures that emerged from the wall more so than wild animals such as tigers and lions. We scattered like frightened sheep in every direction, even clawing at the one and only door to no avail. The door was solid steel and I could not kick it open no matter how hard I tried.

The Reptilian females studied us and then made their choices and pursued the man they had set their eyes and mind on. The four Reptilian females looked similar to each other, almost exact copies, whereas the twelve human women we mated with earlier had different looks, body shapes, and sizes. How the Reptilian females determined which man they would mate with was a mystery. They didn't fight over us, but somehow, they collectively agreed on which one of us they were going to take down to the mat and maul.

The one that picked me was all over me as fast as a whirlwind. The Reptilian female grabbed me by my hair and nearly pulled it out of my head, then slammed me down to the ground as if I were a helpless child. I bounced off the soft floor, and she jumped on top of me like a tiger ripping into its prey and stuck her slimy Reptilian tongue

182

down my throat until I gagged and nearly threw up in her filthy mouth. She swirled her tongue all over my mouth and sealed our lips together with her gooey Reptilian saliva. I couldn't pull loose from her no matter how hard I tried. She wouldn't let me go and whatever she did activated my penises to harden and latch on to her lower two cavities.

I was familiar with some Reptilian species and their peculiar anatomies, breeding behaviors and bizarre prowess but not this Reptilian breed. I knew nothing about them or their mating rituals and revolting customs. I'm certain it was a far different experience when they mated with their kind (Reptilian males) than when they mated with the far less aggressive and weaker humans. I started out human, but the Serpents fed the other men and me Reptilian hormones and testosterone through the tubes mixed in with our food to develop our freakish penises that were in line with Reptilian males. Our bodies remained the same for the most part, it was only our reproductive junk that changed, but I wasn't sure. The Serpents equipped us with Reptilian sexual anatomy designed to perform on both human and Reptilian females. And it seemed to work just fine.

After a few moments of my struggle and her apparent enjoyment, she began to orgasm, and she flailed her arms madly above her head while screeching like a wild cat in heat. I orgasmed before her which trigger her

183

orgasm. Then she began to choke me with her claw-like hands around my throat. She had loosened her suction grip on my lips shortly after she orgasmed and I had hardly caught my breath when she began choking me again. She eventually let go of me and scuttled back into the hole in the wall like the freakish animal that she was.

After being impregnated, the Reptilian females one by one left the room and scurried back into the holes in the wall. Left stunned, I waited impatiently for the Androids to come and let us out of that brutal animal cage. It was a torture chamber like I have never been exposed to before (that I remembered). The Androids took longer to release us from the room than they did the day before, which prolonged my agony.

Ravaged and thrown to the side like used rubbers by the female Reptilians, we crawled back to our beloved sanctuary the barracks, the only place on that wicked ship we found rest and hit the sacks. I had no energy or desire to go to the feeding tubes. Nor did any of the other three men. I was physically sick and would have puked had I the strength. The inside of my mouth was scratched and ripped in places from her abrasive and jagged tongue, and in her lunacy, she chewed away part of my tongue. The taste inside my mouth was that of my blood mixed with the awful and foul Reptilian mucus from her saliva. I wanted badly to go wash out my mouth but lacked the assets or the will to crawl out of my bunk.

Vestiges of my spirit mind survived after my ordeal with the female Reptilian, enough to know intuitively that my situation and predicament was no accident. I dreaded that we were inside of a Reptilian ship flying through space on our way to a Reptilian space colony or one of the Reptilian planets to become a permanent part of their wicked breeding programs that I had heard about.

Days passed, and we were no longer bothered by the Androids, and we laid around doing much of nothing other than staring at the four walls of our prison. For the other humans, that didn't seem to be much of a problem, they were catatonic without mind and functioned on a bare minimum level of consciousness. The Reptilians had wiped their minds of the grotesque memories I was forever stuck with. The other men's minds perhaps had been destroyed, being that the Reptilians were only in need of their bodies to perform certain mundane sexual functions. Apparently, my mind was not susceptible to whatever mind jamming and wiping used on the other men. I envied them, for I wished I could remove the memories of the anguish I had endured with the Serpents and Reptilian females.

REPTILIAN PLANET Z

At some point, we reached our destination, a planet out somewhere in the darkness of endless space. I had no idea what star system it was. I wasn't picking up the signals that would tell me precisely my location, due to the fact I remained trapped inside of a physical Reptilian and partly modified human body. The physical aspect shielded and distorted much of my ability to navigate through the cosmos, inherent in higher-echelon spirit beings. There was no doubt in my mind, after my ordeal, that I was, in fact, a fallen spirit, recast in the physical realm of one of the many levels of Hades.

The Androids showed up at our barracks one day, and for the first time, I was glad to see them. I had experienced the equivalent of solitary confinement for months, perhaps years; unable to communicate with any of the human vegetables that shared the barracks with me created a hole in my mind and soul. The Androids, three of them, escorted the human group of men, my group, and other groups located elsewhere that we had no contact with, to some place off the ship. I alone was taken to a place in the opposite direction by one of the Androids.

We arrived at a Reptilian and Serpent planet, not a space colony or barren moon as I originally expected. The city was massive, and looking down from the top of a huge skyscraper that reached near the edge of space from where the ship docked, I was impressed and flabbergasted with what I saw. I had seen Reptilian settlements on various moons but haven't learned much about them because they are extremely picky about what gets out about them. Serpents, more so than Reptilians, are very effective at keeping their existence under the radar and ruthless in their dealings with those who would violate their concealed presence, exterminating and killing anything or anyone with the ability to blabber about Serpent secrecies.

I knew I was in danger because of who I am. I'm a spirit being that collects as much information about anything and everything I come across during my galactic voyages in the cosmos. Why the Reptilians and Serpents would even conceive of bringing me into their coveted secret hive, on their planet, made no sense, unless they had no intentions of letting me leave or live. My power was in my spirit form, not my corporeal shell, which they could not control me in totality once I became a spirit. But they could keep me alive in my physical body for as long as they wished, a thought that terrified the hell out of me.

I walked off the ship and was led by the Android onto a massive platform overlooking much of the city below. The Android left me there without speaking a word and returned to the ship. The platform was hemispherical and made of a glass-type material that enveloped the platform. From the platform, I had a crystal-clear view of space above and the glowing, magnificent, humongous crystal city below. Skyscrapers from the city jetted up over the landscape as far as my physical eyes could see, and I could see quite a distance from my perch on the platform. The city was mesmerizing and beautiful, glittering with pulsating colors and variously lit up and sparkling buildings. I was awestruck and perplexed that the barbaric despicable Reptilian beings I had contact with on the ship had any association with such a spectacular and vibrant city/planet.

The sun (star), a giant star that could swallow hundreds if not thousands of yellow stars as the one Earth belongs to, was prominent in the sky and taking up a large portion of the view from the planet I was on. I was not familiar with this star or the hundreds of billions of other stars which I had yet to explore in this sector, assuming I was still in my sector. Looking at the star rejuvenated my spirit that was rotting inside of my physical monstrosity of half-human and part-Reptilian beast of a body.

The Reptilian planet was one of the innermost planets in that star system and up-close and cozy with the massive star. Several moons and moonlets of various sizes, colors and designs were clearly visible and remarkable in their orbits around that planet.

I have never tired of the cosmic wonders that I have been privileged to witness and experience firsthand during my existence. The cosmos, at no time, has ceased to amaze me even while in the depths of misery as I am now. The raw uniqueness of every star and planetary systems within each star, was magical food for weary souls as mine. And my soul had never been exhausted as it was now. I knew not which star system or what this planet might be called and, at that time, didn't know if I would ever be allowed to know or behold such wonders again, should the Serpents imprison me in one of their infinite number of dungeons under the surface of that planet. I knew that much about the Serpents; they held the keys to many types of prisons for isolating whomever they wished and for whatever reasons, in the cosmic sectors where they operated and controlled.

I was alone on the platform which was odd. It was a very large platform that could hold hundreds of sightseers, or dignitaries or sex-slaves or prisoners awaiting to be locked up down on that planet. The other humans that I cohabitated with for a long, arduous stretch of time were taken down to the city in elevators that were visible from the platform. They didn't get to go on the platform and marvel at the city below as I was allowed to do, perhaps because they were zombies with little or no mind left to be able to appreciate fantastic things and sights. I knew not what fate laid in wait for them, or myself, on this Reptilian planet and did not envy them. Somehow, I knew I wasn't doomed to remain on this planet much longer, but that, being only wishful hoping.

After a few moments of being on the platform, a Serpent entered the platform and walked towards me. It was not the same type of Serpent that terrorized me on the ship inside the copulating room; they, slithered like snakes as in a pit of vipers. This Serpent was humanoid and about the same height as I was, six-feet tall. The Serpent wore a three-piece suit and looked very professional. The Serpent talked my language, or I talked its language, whatever it was, we understood each other perfectly and vocally. The Serpent sounded human and displayed human mannerisms and characteristics. I also knew, from past travels, that some Serpents mimic every detail of the beings they encounter. This Serpent might have been such a creature, and such an encounter for the Serpent was very cordial, polite and highly intelligent. However, his face was not human but the shape of a snake's face, oval and smooth with hints of scales.

The Serpent said he was aware of who I was, a spirit being from one of the Eropmanop stars. And that it was no accident that they captured me, it was intentional. They wanted my specific seed, physical and spirit seed, my offspring, in their massive collection of physical beings.

I was not the first of my kind that they had captured and taken seed from, he told me and that it was a common practice to capture spirit beings while they frolicked in physical bodies on planets and moons as I was doing.

That revelation was bothersome to me because I knew I had no power from preventing the scheme forced upon me. He then, without hesitation and that caught me by complete surprise, slit my throat with one swift move of his clawed hand, and I dropped like a sack of potatoes, onto the platform floor suffocating on my blood gushing out of my mortally-wounded body. I was bleeding profusely and laid dying on the cold metal platform flopping around like a chicken with its head chopped off, and I died. The Serpent said, "you are welcome," and walked off the platform and into a stairwell that led to a bank of elevators and took one of the elevators down to the city below. I saw the whole thing, the crime scene, and was floating above my carcass, freed from my human/Reptilian corpse at last!

I had been trapped inside that physical perversion hybrid contraption of a body for nearly a year or more and now, freed from it. I was happy again, a feeling I had been deprived of for all those horrible months in Reptilian captivity. I was joyous, and I immediately flew to the elevator that the Serpent was in and said: "Thank You!" And he repeated, "You are welcome." He asked me if I planned to stay long in his city, on his planet? I told him I would like to see and know more about the city if there were no objections. He gave me his approval and permission, which allowed me more leeway than I could ever have hoped to achieve under any other situation. I flew out of the elevator and into the city to explore it and add my experience of the Serpent planet to Eropmanop through my sidekick Pi.

Pi had hovered around me like a lost puppy the whole time during my imprisonment but was unable to assist me or contact me. I knew Pi was there even though I was hardly aware of Pi's presence at my side. I learned additional tricks of the trade that I employed immediately to keep from falling into future traps by sly beings as the Serpents and Reptilians. And I admonished Pi to be diligent on my behalf and for my welfare for the times that I wasn't. However, I had no illusions of my being foolproof and had a new appreciation of the super powers Serpents and some Reptilian breeds possessed in both the physical and spirit realms. I would forever be cautious and attentive whenever I was around Serpents and Reptilians, more so if I suspected they be in the area of my interest during my casual interactions in the corporal domains.

The Reptilian city covered a large portion of the planet, and one other city, a Serpent city, covered the rest of the planet. Only two cities on a planet fifty times the size of Earth. No vegetation worth noting existed on the planet's exterior surface. There was no surface water, lakes, rivers, seas or oceans. But the planet did have huge reserves of subsurface water. The planet was hot, too hot for human habitation without protective suits. The oxygen levels were too low for humans without protective outfits and gear. The Reptilian city was a maze of metal and glass structures with various sizes and shapes of buildings. Sidewalks and streets didn't exist. Hospitals, schools, prisons, zoos, parks, museums or any public conveniences and fun destinations were absent from the Reptilian city.

A segregated planet split down the middle with the Serpents occupying one side of the planet and a pure-breed and distinctive race of Reptilians, a far different breed than other types of Reptilians that I had encountered in the past, took up the other part of the planet. The planet was stationary, without rotation and the Serpent portion of the planet faced the sun and the dark side of the planet the Reptilian half. Serpents were the dominant breed on the planet and had many administrative offices within the Reptilian city. The two cities were as different as night and day (no pun intended).

The Reptilian cityscape of buildings and skyscrapers reminded me of layers of multi-colored jagged massive glass and crystal shards pointing principally upwards to the sky but also every which way, a chaotic architectural design, yet very pleasantly colorful, inspiring,

193

stirring and mind-challenging. The Serpent city, in contrast, was more reserved, conservative, with a uniformed low-rise and attractive stately buildings, which covered the landscape like a fine tapestry of exquisitely embroidered gold. The Serpent city was a massive city made of solid yellow gold.

Neither of the cities had animals, domestic or wild, no birds or sea life, or flying and crawling insects within their municipalities. However, deep in the underground section of the Serpent city every kind of beast, animal, humanoid and otherwise was there in massive quantities. Also, infinite numbers of insects for purposes I was not allowed to know. Both cities were immense jewels mounted onto the planet like precious colorful and intriguing stones, well organized and arranged, immaculate, sparkly and squeaky clean.

Reptilians and Serpents had fanciful and exquisite dining facilities, restaurants, eateries, cafeterias, for lack of more descriptive words for their magnificent eating establishments. Reptilians and Serpents treated food consumption on the same level as religious institutions and equating food to things of worship. Eateries on both sides of the planet were superb, but the Serpents' food places were like the cathedrals in European cities with unbelievable ornate grottos, altars, statues, pillars and columns with massive quantities of delicately crafted adornments. Serpents and to a lesser extent the Reptilians, worshiped the food they ate and more so the places they dined. The Serpents adored and surrounded themselves with the magnificent and majestic atmosphere in the areas they lived, worked and consumed food.

Office buildings, high rise apartments (living quarters) for the Reptilians was a huge contrast in living space and style compared to where and how the Serpents lived. The Reptilians lived on the other side of the tracks, where housing was modest rowhouses, apartments and condo type structures that took up most of the high-rise buildings in the Reptilian city. No single-family houses and more like beehives, pads and such. They had a variety of domiciles. Nothing extravagant, but their housing was clean, adequately functional and pleasant. Considering what types of beings Reptilians were, their lives seemed over the top and well organized. I had presumed that they lived in caves like wild animals, as was true with some other races of Reptilians I've known and dealt with in the past.

Serpents loved the high life and all the bells and whistles that came with super-rich living arrangements. Serpents lived inside of massively ornate mansions with exquisite details in what appeared to be finely crafted exotic hardwoods imported from planets in star systems from around the galaxies. No mansion was like another mansion; each Serpent Castle was a unique jewel inside a setting of marvelously manicured gardens decorated with fountains, waterfalls, and streams. Billions upon billions of such magnificent estates existed on the Serpents' side of the tracks.

The mansions and their gardens were inside of covered buildings, buildings made of solid gold and topped with glassed roofs that filtered the sunlight and other radiation deemed unsuitable to the Serpents but mostly their prized exotic flowering florae. Mind-numbing varieties of flowering plants I have never set eyes on, in all my cosmic travels in the universe. I've only seen a small fraction of what exists in my corner of the universe but the Serpent city, with its many unusual surprises at every turn, the very few turns they allowed me to take, will be near impossible to beat.

Replicators created all the food (that I was aware of) and every possible dish for Reptilian and Serpent appetites, which were unexpectedly sophisticated and diverse. Reptilians and the Serpents, at least those on this planet, are remarkably cultured and astute beings, the Serpents more so than the Reptilians.

Not plagued by wars, famine or disease, the Reptilians certainly understood the intricacies of dishing that stuff out to other inhabitants and races on other planets and moons, in the galactic regions they overshadowed.

Attire was Reptilian skin that was leathery and nothing more did they wear. The Serpents' skin was smoother and softer than the Reptilians' skin. The Serpent that slashed my throat projected onto me, my human mind before slaying me, human attire. When in fact, the Serpent wore no clothing and was in a natural state when I viewed him in the elevator in my spirit form. Serpents dress or give the appearance of wearing apparel when they are around cultured humans, those who tend to be offended when around nude savages.

Humans at higher levels of existence were not offended by nakedness as those living in lower level planets. Upper bracket humans were also not cannon fodder for perverse Serpent dealings and morbid modifications by Reptilians. But they were not completely under the Serpent's radar either. There was plenty evidence on the Serpent planet that multiple strata of humans and subhuman types played many roles of mysterious purposes that went far beyond the mating and reproduction scheme I had gotten a taste. They, the humans and non-humans, had other reasons for being on the Serpent planet that I was not privy to and possibly never would be; at least, the whole picture for me remained skewed.

Reptilians and Serpents don't consume alcoholic beverages or take drugs or stimulants, not even coffee, tea or cocoa or other exotic Alien drinks designed to dull or excite the senses. Reptilians procreate feverishly and spread their kind in a frenzy of activity coming on like a plague of locust and embed their progeny on fertile planets and star systems, from where they will, on some future date, harvest and reap what they have sowed. Literally and not metaphorically.

Sex is common and constant, primarily with the Reptilians, but the Serpents have equal time in the sack, for pleasure mostly. Serpents don't procreate nearly as much or as often as the Reptilians. Lifespan is longer with the Serpents than with the Reptilians, by a hundred or more earth years. After which the Serpents renew, without having to reincarnate, if they so desire. Some chose to end their lives and reenter through the birth canal of life, which is rare. Reptilians, of the species on this planet, live for hundreds of years, five, six hundred or more. And they spread their spawn rapidly throughout the star systems and then give up their carcasses to the cosmic whims of space. In space, Reptilian corpses continue the process of spawning when captured by gravitational fields of planets and moons, which then get pollinated with a Reptilian product like a sugar dusting on pastries. Once that happens, the sugar coating becomes a base for future Reptilian races to grow.

Reptilians masquerade as other types of star beings and creatures when they invade planets, to better infiltrate and facilitate their will on the humanoid societies. Often, the scam consists of showing concern for planetary ecosystems and other political subterfuge used as a dividing and disabling strategy that leads to controlling and subjugating subordinate species, in the humanoid categories. Political systems are similar and prevalent on many star systems throughout the galaxy, since the same overlords ruled over multiple planetary systems as franchises. Like hamburger and fried chicken franchise restaurants, they have the same food menu and choices wherever you go.

Reptilian souls are an anomaly that I was unable to crack fully. They have souls, a life force within their carcasses that animates them but lacks an ethical predisposition, as their human cousins strive towards but also lack. Humans have a quest, even though most don't know it or understand what that quest is. A human quest to reach higher ground in the cosmic order, the heaven and hell syndrome. Humans, search and long for unity and community, while holding tightly to a security-blanket and obsessive neediness, in a universe that instead propels souls towards maturity, individuality and eventual autonomy (kicked out of the nest). A rude awakening for most humans when they die and realize that is what it's all about, growing up and moving on to better things and becoming adults.

Reptilians have no such quest or delusions, and they exist for a known purpose, one that they fully understand and comprehend. Reptilians lack the full spectrum of emotions and have no mood swings from happy to sad or sad to happy. They are what they are and need not search for answers to why they are or for what purpose they exist. Reptilians exist, and that's the end of it as far as they are concerned. No discussion will change that reality.

Serpents are a far different animal than Reptilians when it comes to souls. Serpents have a strong everlasting soul, and they are fully aware of their soul even while in corporal uniform. Unlike humans, who aren't sure they have a soul or what a soul is, if they do have one. Serpents have incarnated into Serpent beings from the realms of the spirits, ripe and ready to go from day one. Serpents don't have baby Serpents (often), but it can and does happen under strange rituals and circumstances (the details, withheld from me). Serpents have spirit-souls that have originated at the higher echelon of ethereal beings, from much higher places than my Eropmanop soul. Serpents choose to enter the physical zones and come and go at their leisure, morphing from one to the other routinely. Serpents can park their carcasses (bodies), leave and return whenever they want, to their original bodies or create new bodies, or never again enter the physical realms as Serpents or anything else.

I discovered that I was much more active during my time on the Reptilian ship than I knew while on the ship. Pi continued recording every moment of my life while on the ship and in the modified Reptilian human body. I had believed that I was left in the barracks to do nothing other than count the days of my incarceration with the other men. The Reptilians changed the material that came through the feeding tubes more often than I realized. They had placed me into a zombie state like what the other men existed in. It took them longer to figure out the correct formula that worked on me to block and thwart my mental faculties.

The orgies continued and became far more bizarre as other types of beings were introduced into the mixture. These were not lascivious and pleasure orgies for me and the other human men, and mercifully, they blanked out most of the dreadful details while it happened. I was now aware of all that happened and took place at the behest of the Serpents, who orchestrated the daily ordeals. Details placed into the files, I keep on Eropmanop and not revealed in this document. The main thrust of the ordeals was to impregnate females of numerous species that the Serpents farmed and brought to life throughout this quadrant of the cosmos run by them. Most of the females were humanoid types of creations, but the Serpents also had various animal species that they fermented into the mixture and to be used in early (new) civilizations that they had under their charge.

I fathered, without my knowledge or consent, untold numbers of offspring for the use in old and new startup civilizations throughout the quadrant. I did a lot of that on my own before the Reptilians captured me, but I raised and participated on some level with the upbringing of my offspring and had plenty of personal contact with my children. That was not the case with what the Serpents involved me in. But in the Serpent manifesto, I would be allowed to know whatever I wished to know about my offspring that were scattered in the far corners of this quadrant, if I so desired to have a relationship with any of them, even the animal ones.

As far as I was concerned, the Reptilians I mated with were as wild of animals as animals can be, but so are all physical beings, humanoids and humans too, simply another breed of animal species inside the animal kingdom of the physical realms in this universe. Certain types of animals such as humans, are endowed, uploaded, with software, metaphorically speaking, that gave humans smarts and a low level of awareness (consciousness). But all animals have been given intelligence and speech on various planets including earth-type planets during early stages of planetary development.

The physical part of the universe is a wild kingdom for those stuck in the muck of the lower physical realms and left with the little memory of how much muck one treads through before they are let out and allowed to join the spirit world on some level.

The men who were made to be like zombies, and later myself too, were in fact implanted with other types of souls during our tribulations as slaves to the Reptilians and their arbitrary expertise in lower realm matters. Our souls subordinated to souls who took over our minds and bodies for the purpose of infusing semen with the invading souls' spirit elements. The other men being supplanted by other souls did not inseminate the women with their soul material as I did when I was fully conscious during my copulations. The offspring from the encounters had the physical genes of the men and the spiritual genes of the soul that inhabited them during copulation. What or who these "other" souls were, remained a mystery to me and belongs to that mountainous pile of information that remained forever forbidden knowledge. At least for me and the level I resided at now, in my lengthy stage of awakening.

SERPENT GOLDEN CITIES

The Serpent city is a city of massive wealth, where most everything is gold-infused if not pure gold. Everything is of gold, buildings, inside and out, even the exquisitely unusual furniture and decor used by the Serpents is of gold, mixed with other precious metals and materials.

Golden low-rise buildings of various heights, all connected and that covered millions of square miles in every direction, encrusted the planet facing the massive star. Every inch of the Serpent-half of the planet had woven into the golden landscape, Serpent themes, designs and fantastic, animated features that energized the surface of every inch of the living and working spaces of the Serpent residents. Serpents busied themselves with many types of strange activities, all at once. I was unable to decipher much of what they were doing, as it was a jumbled mass of confusion for my level of awareness to comprehend.

My awareness is extremely high and off-the-charts, compared with the level of the typical human awareness, yet I could not keep up with the Serpents' sophisticated manner of mind play and manipulation of how they did things while performing projects. Multi-tasking at lightspeed on a slow day is but one facet of thousands of facets

Serpents own and put on display. There was no cracking the nut of what Serpents were. That was one reason I was allowed in their midst; they understood that I could not figure them out and, therefore, it was safe to allow me to look around some of the city. Serpents are an anomaly like no other, by their imaginative engineering. Serpents are anomalies that change constantly and swiftly every second of their existence (everything about them changes). There was no way to break their code since everything they were from one minute to the next left no traces to pick through, decipher and catalogue. For this written report, I have had to fill in many pieces of the puzzle using my deductive skills, which the Serpents allowed me.

On the Reptilian side of the planet, the stars, planets, and moons were as large as ripe fruit hanging down from clear night skies. Reptilians had no daylight and were perpetually on the dark side of the planet but had a view of the starlight (sun) that reflected down from the many bright moons in the night sky. Reptilians had massively tall buildings, skyscrapers from where they could catch a glimpse of the star the planet orbited from, the very tips of some of the outlying tall buildings on the edges, near the side of the planet facing the star. Reptilians had space cities, some that connected directly to the planet from spaceports and from where they had spectacular views of the star. The Reptilian city glowed multicolored and created no glare to obstruct the nighttime view of the splendid night sky. The planet had no surface water and no weather and therefore no cloudy nights. Solar heat from the Serpent side of the planet was collected by the golden buildings and conducted through the planet and provided heat and energy to the Reptilians residing on the dark side of the planet.

Serpent buildings rose above the ground not more than fifty feet but extended deep underground in the expanded subterranean city that continued substantially under the surface and reaching down into the core of the planet. I wasn't allowed to go to the deepest parts of the underground city where the Serpents hid their most valued secrets of their highly covert enterprises. The whole Serpent structure exceeded billions of square feet of solid gold and other, equally if not more exotic, materials. The amount of gold used to construct the massive city that covered half of the planet was astronomical, considering that more than haft the planet's interior was part of the Serpent city. Serpents had the means and know-how of making and weaving gold (and anything else they needed or wanted to create). Serpent gold is the gold found on many planets, moons and rocks throughout the quadrant including Earth.

Labyrinths and inexplicable mazes incorporated into the city for the use of the Serpents and their guests, willing and unwilling guests, housed and kept in the furthest and remotest depths of the city. Guests were any number of races and beings that the Serpents had dealings with and operated through or subjugated and warehoused. The humans on the ship with me during the sexcapades are now permanent "guests" somewhere inside the massive bowels of the Serpent city.

I was not escorted around the city and had no one to query answers from, for the myriad of questions I had about the Serpents. Questions I knew the Serpents would not answer. I was on my own and had to deduce information about what I saw and what I would be allowed to comprehend, even if shown to me. I understood the danger I put myself in by going into the lion's den, where one slip and I could find myself trapped indefinitely inside anyone of the many mysterious labyrinths and mazes with their countless nefarious dungeons. The Serpents had captured me once in my physical form, that I'm aware of, and they certainly had abilities to capture my soul and detain it if they had reason or no reason at all for as long as they wished.

Lesser types and breeds of Serpents existed who also harbored highly mysterious elements of their being, but nothing like this class of Serpents I was now absorbed in, and looking for the innermost secrets and hints of what made them tick. This class of Serpent was the apex of the

Serpent societies and untouchable by other powers in the upper ends of the spirit realms. I was, for a time, entrenched inside one of many hidden valleys of the abyss under the Serpent city that held information about one of the powerful pillars behind the curtain of movers and shakers of cosmic empires.

I could not infer the number of Serpents in the city other than a visual and I did see millions of them, even though much of the city seemed filled with empty buildings and colossal vacant spaces with no hint of their intended purpose. The Serpent city, built like a machine, is a massive, printed circuit with billions of layers upon billions of layers of thick strata of gold. The sheets of gold separated by air, noble gasses and numerous other unique and strange liquids, minerals, and metals that I had not seen before, or will most likely ever have the opportunity to see again.

Some parts of the city were used as holding pens for different types of beings and creatures corralled inside rooms, between layers of floors throughout the underground. Rooms inside of the buildings, inside of labyrinths, inside of mazes, inside of jumbles and tangles of webs, had many diverse physical dimensions, shapes, and sizes designed to accommodate and fit peculiar occupants placed in the holding pens.

I didn't see any vile things going on while there, and the creatures and other beings I caught glimpses of didn't appear distressed. But I also only saw a fraction of the Serpent machinery and its myriad of occupants inside compartments of the apparatus. Most of the city existed at extreme subterranean levels and cloaked in mysterious darkness, blocked off to my inquisitive and prying mind. I, therefore, could not make a clear judgment of what the Serpents were and were doing. Only clues did I have. But clues are not information suitable for Eropmanop and therefore of little use.

I was a spirit, a ghost to the multitudes of beings and creatures I surveyed on the Serpent planet during my investigations of the massively clandestine Serpent city. Only the Serpents and Reptilians could pick up on my presence inside of their domains and cities. The Serpents possess a keen sense of telepathy, and a mastery of the paranormal like few other beings in this part of the universe can claim. The Serpents had the upper hand when dealing with most realities of spirit and physical forms and me, only a gnat in comparison to many of the other beings they had dealings with. I could apply many of the techniques the Serpents did, shapeshift, and change from spirit to physical on a whim, but Serpents captured me and showed me who had the better tricks up their sleeves. I'm aware of only a smattering of the Serpents' mindboggling and mind-blocking techniques that superseded and surpassed paranormal perplexities familiar to me and other spirit servants inside the great halls of cosmic knowledge and wisdom.

INTANGIBLE BEINGS

I was not a trickster, at least not malicious, in my treatment of subordinate beings. I entered the physical world for my personal enjoyment and to propagate my progeny and species, as was expected of my kind to do by the higher cosmic beings. I fooled the women I mated with into believing I was a human as they were, and remained within the lines governing duty-bound projects. Humans I engaged during my travels in the physical worlds had no reason to doubt or suspect something was amiss when I entered their lives for whatever reasons, because nothing was amiss but sanctioned by the powers that be. The spirit beings, sprites and any number of exotic creatures as myself, have always indulged in dalliances with beings in physical abodes that are stuck and frozen inside of time-spheres harnessed to the physical realms by personal weaknesses and failures. Physicality is not much different than the tar pits that held vulnerable, and soon-to-be-mutilated animals caught in devious plots by the tar.

Humanoid beings have handicapped awareness levels and fail to grasp the realities of myriads of paranormal creatures that regularly infest and interfere with them from the moment of birth into the physical realm until the last breath before death, only to enter a period of confusion (for some) between realities for a time. Then, scuttled back to the physical realm for yet another crack at embodiment. Some souls escape the round trips and are allowed to pass from confusion, into an area of vast new awareness available only to those in the spirit realms.

Some human souls can enter my unique dominion of existence and become spirit species as myself and be forever free of reincarnation (For the most part). For, as I have discovered, paranormal tricksters abound and can infringe on freedoms, for those who continue to dabble in the physical dominions rather than take leave of the physical boneyard, forever. Even Serpent powers over me will abate at some point, at higher levels that I have yet to reach, but I know I am near that threshold. I have remained duty-bound to Eropmanop for reasons I have since fulfilled and can choose to exit this physical universe and enter other spirit-friendly dimensions and universes anytime I choose.

When humans enter that land of confusion, if they are not so inclined to remain there by deep-rooted fears of entering the unknown cosmos, and have the compulsory qualities demanded from Eropmanop, they can find an entry point. Once found and passed through, they can become a new type of soul from where they can earn a path towards full autonomy, and enjoy freedoms reserved for spiritual cosmic gods.

I exist in a realm of the infinite pursuit of exploration, exclusively of my desires and design. I cross paths with the things considered fairy tales and fables by human souls who are underdeveloped and lacking in awareness of the cosmic energy around them. Only a small percentage of paranormal and ethereal beings have made themselves known to the human world, as fairies, elves, leprechauns, trolls, gnomes, sprites, which are only a few of the inhabitants and occupants of the mythical creation that occasionally steps on Earth-type planets. Many kinds of spirit beings and creatures, playing, plotting, scheming, proliferating, circulating, fornicating and dancing with each other, and with the lucky few humans gifted with their cognizance. Such creatures are "real," versus the irrational and baseless delusions that are called "tangibles", by the vast and unwashed masses of humanity throughout the galaxy.

In the history of human populations on Earth, throughout the world of early times, living in ancient history had one thing in common, they worshiped multitudes of gods and other invisible beings. Gods represented specialties and possessed keen abilities to bring certain aspects of desires to life, and make them realities for those poor human souls who called on their gods for help and clarity. Hundreds and thousands of such gods worked diligently to make things happen for those who believed in them and for those who didn't.

Prayers asking for a change in the weather and many other types of requests by people to the gods, rose into the sky like billowing clouds: "make it warm, bring on the rain, let my crops prosper, save my ailing hog, horse, sheep, dog, donkey, etc. Keep my hens safe from ravaging foxes and other predators. Make my wife, husband, children well again. Look after this and look after that." These were not and are not idol prayers and requests to the invisible, non-existent gods; they were and are, fervent appeals to beings who were and are real and more tangible than the tangibles in the physical domains. Such creatures back then and still now, listen and always respond to requests and prayers. However, all responses come with conditions that will be met, like peeling a banana before one can enjoy the fruit inside. Some people object to having to peel the banana to get to the fruit. They are the ones not ready to forgo the merry-go-round and madness of the physical world they exist inside—the tar pit.

Superstitions based on the same realities, as past and present deities remain intangible to the most gullible and naive in the society of humans. In other words, those people who need the most proof concerning the "supernatural" are, in fact, the naivest, believing only in what they can see, taste or touch. Such depth of unknowing is at the rudimentary level of awareness that even wild animals surpass. I, too, have been in the basement of massive denial and ignorance of the unseen world that is more real than the seen world while a human on Earth. Gratefully, my moment of naiveté hasn't blocked me from entering and receiving near full-blown awareness of the cosmos, as I have now.

Some humans are far more in tune with the real existence, which is never physical existence, than other humans. People believe in things because down, deep inside, they "know," they remember bits of their origins in the spirits realms. They, or someone they know or have known, had their wishes and desires looked after and responded to, which clued them and confirmed to them the bogus that is the physical and so-called tangible world.

The awareness-challenged people demand that only tangibles be on their dinner plates in a restaurant (the world) created, filled, and run by intangible spirit beings and creatures. I am an intangible spirit being, and I cross paths with numerous other intangible beings, and we sometimes sit and chat about how wonderfully tangible we are. We listen, and we hear, the cries and wishes of the billions of souls entangled inside of flesh and blood ignorance. We hear the moans, the screams, the wishes and hopes and we respond in due time and appropriately to each and every one of them. But we spirit beings, never peel a banana for anyone (unless they ask nicely). That would be a disservice to them if we did and liability and a handicap they would have to learn to live with, during potentially additional multiple lives in the physical realms.

Spirit beings often peel away the illusions now and then and let those stuck in the muck of the physical world see a glimpse, a tease, a taste of the real stuff, the intangible stuff that is the stuff of the wondrous cosmos. We of the spirit realm, know more about the needs of the people than the people know about themselves or their exclusively unique needs and wants. And we provide the best remedy that fits each unique situation known and experienced by man, woman, and child, who cry out for help and guidance.

Help happens to all living souls in the sewage of human situations, whether they ask for help or not. Help seldom is appreciated due that it comes at a price: a change of attitude, a change of diet, a change of job, spouse or lifestyle. Painful changes seldom are welcomed, and the grumbling continues on the billions of Earth-type planets in most galaxies in this universe.

I might step in and offer a solution to a problem that an unsuspecting person struggles over. I might not stick around to see if my advice has a positive or negative resolution. Other spirits might step in and give their two-bits and move on also. Some spirits will stick it out to the end and make sure their advice is heeded, acted on and implemented, and bring it to a happy ending no matter how much pain it takes to get to the happy ending. There will always be a spirit being to pick up the ball when the ball gets dropped by the human or humans and any number of spirit beings that choose to move in and move on. Humans are never alone, not even for a nanosecond. Some pesky sprite is always nearby and ready to kiss a boo-boo, crack the whip or place a boot up a derriere.

Spirit beings don't work alone when responding to requests and prayers, they frequently use and incorporate things that are already in people's lives, like pets, friends, relatives and strangers and bring them into the quest for a resolution. Resolutions can be immediate or take on a life of their own, as they work behind the scenes to bring about and manifest solutions, for difficult changes to fall into place. Some are lengthy processes that can take months, years and lifetimes to achieve before being put to rest.

SERPENTS

The reality of the physical dominions is that they are the spawning grounds of material existence. Every living thing exists primarily to procreate and spread its progeny by whatever means suitable and practical. It's the way life in the physical realms continued to flourish and proliferate in a never-ending state of presence. Flora and fauna are designed to exist in a constant, propagating mode from which keeps ecological systems throughout the galaxies and the universe, crawling, jumping, flying, squirming and for the human contemplators, postulating.

Reptilians play a major role in the propagation of life on the lower cosmic planets, moons, and realms. Humans too, without knowing the full extent of their cosmic involvement. Most people are awash in sports, religion, games, politics, and any number of distraction designed by the overlords to skew the view of what lies behind the cosmic curtain hiding the massive reproduction and other planetary and spacefaring activities humans participate in daily, mostly without their knowledge.

Serpents and their underlings manufacture much of the elements that make up the physical realms on planets and moons where humans mostly reside. Serpents engineer and create the creatures, animals, insects, and bacteria of the human worlds. Serpents create the tangible physical things that are the illusions that generate the delusions humans cocoon inside (personal bubbles).

Serpents deliver the goods requisitioned by gods and overlords to populate their planetary domains with unique and exotic flora and fauna, for some of the special planets; and the basic everyday flora and fauna for the run-of-the-mill planets like Earth.

Down, deep inside the caverns of Serpent cities on Serpent planets, which number in the billions across the universe, are the hidden forges, where beasts of every kind imaginable, get pounded into existence like fine steel inside of a cosmic blacksmith shop. Every microbe, insect, animal, humanoid, and human are forged and tested and tweaked, before being sent to their assigned new homes on planets and moons. On arrival, testing and tweaking continue indefinitely for all biological-based life forms, plant, and animal. Each planet and moon, no matter how similar to other planets and moons, retain elements of uniqueness in types of genes, physics, and the category of matter found on them. Lifeforms are manufactured and made to adapt to the places destined to exist on.

Serpents and cohorts, Reptilians, set up shop, building outlandish compounds and villages on the planets where they place material, physical creations. Creations by Serpents and further manipulated into the culture of their offspring after many levels of trials and further adaptations to propagate. Crossbreeding with natives of beings from earlier startups on the planetary system and other startups from adjoining planetary systems, are part of the evolutionary process of biological lifeforms, administered by the Serpents and their staff.

Hindered from going deep inside the Serpent city where the magic of physical life gets forced into existence, I was nevertheless allowed to behold some of the procedures taking place once the biological material got further handled on a newer planetary system. Serpents granted me a small peak of the primeval, of the primordial process.

Serpent-Androids created and built magnificent structures of various sizes and shapes, that were both above ground and far below ground, on a vast scale on countless planets and moons. They used mostly available stones quarried in nearby mines and far-off mines. What was obtainable within a certain range of each project, ended up in the project. Limestone, granite, marble, quartz and any number of other local stones, became the makings of mind and body-altering structures for modifying and tweaking humanoid awareness. Such structures had limited time spans for operation, before succumbing to the ravages of weather, floods, earthquakes, battles, and other kinds of natural and unnatural, supernatural upheavals. For those reasons and slews of other objectives, structures continually got repaired and sometimes expanded, destroyed or expunged from the land completely. Less important structures got decommissioned and abandoned, left for the scavengers from succeeding epochs, for use as building materials.

Such structures were primary mockups, that would repeat over millennia and longer periods of millions of years when humanoids transitioned to other epochs of subsequent generations. Humanoid projects that started over again and again, between periods of dormancy to allow rest for the planets.

Stone structures varied in size, scope, and shape. Often, most of the structure was hidden below the surface buildings and out of sight and mind of the original humanoids, who were the reason and the purpose for the large constructs and buildings. Hidden places that remain out of sight and mind of the more advanced human societies that emerged from the original humanoids of the past. Pyramids and other formations of rock-work of every conceivable size and shape are, foremost, of types of stone that covered sections of the planet's surface and a considerable amount of space beneath the structures. As well as above the structures and into the stratosphere, connected by advanced machinery and materials long since removed and left without a trace, when the projects and programs came to completion and abandoned.

Below the pyramids were, and some segments remain, massive undertakings of mazes and tunnels that ran hundreds and even thousands of miles in every direction, that connected underground chambers on many levels, some miles deep below the surface. Cavernous chambers, natural and constructed by Serpent Androids, using highly sophisticated and technologically complex, paranormal machinery. Many tunnels were part of aquifers, for water used for activities created by the Serpents and also for drainage systems to remove excess water from saturating parts of the maze, during periods of flooding above and below ground.

Colonies of Reptilian beings built cities inside the caverns and remained hidden to the surface populations of humanoids, humans and extraterrestrial beings from competing planets, moons, and space cities local to this star system and other star systems in the quadrant. The underground cities were once, and some still are, a constant flurry of activities that involved any number of humans, humanoids, and beings from other planets in the star system. Reptilian laboratories were part of the underground cities but were not for experimentation purposes on humans or other biological microbes, animals and plant life. Reptilians didn't experiment, they only performed duties prescribed to them by the Serpents, who dished out orders and commands to the Reptilians.

However, some other types of extraterrestrials that managed to infest Serpent territories, sometimes allowed by the Serpents, performed experiments on humans for various reasons that suited biological needs, as grafting and spawning for their clans. Some breeds of Reptilians fell into that category of renegade villains. When captured they were terminated by any number of the multitudes of servants working for the Serpents and safeguarding human nurseries. Sometimes, even the insurgents with prior permission, who overstayed assigned periods, were exterminated after the completion of programs.

PYRAMIDS

High above the pyramids, several feet above the apex, hovered massive Reptilian and Serpent transport ships, themselves pyramid-shaped. The ships folded over the polished-stone pyramids and became an additional covering over the entire pyramid, encasing the pyramid inside the Serpent ship. Few human leaders in the know about space beings as the Serpents, remained unaware of the phenomenon of the covering and cloaking of the pyramids by Alien ships. Common humans never noticed the folding and unfolding of the Serpent ships during the darkness of night or even during daylight hours.

The Alien ship covering the pyramids had a chameleon effect on the pyramids, that changed colors and even appearances of the pyramids. The ships also acted as a camouflage that hid (cloaked) the pyramids from other hostile stellar beings that had broken through interstellar or planetary defenses. Like huge octopuses, the Alien ships took on many transformations in color, texture, and shape that blended perfectly with the surroundings to hide structures and other activities. Pyramid Alien ships joined with other Alien ships and instantly cloaked whole cities behind impenetrable camouflage that looked like the surrounding terrain, whether it was sand or forest. If and when parts of the city were detected, the Alien ships provided substantial firepower while keeping the whole of the Alien city under its defensive umbrella.

Strange aerial marvels were not uncommon in ancient times, but few humans cared about such extravagant displays by the gods (whom they feared) and ignored and spoke not of the many dealings between gods, for fear of reprisals by the all-powerful and all-knowing Serpent gods. Similar extravagances were occasionally displayed by the human leaders and priests to enforce their authority over the human masses. "Mind your own business and live another day" was the norm for the mortal human and humanoid commoners.

Selected pyramids were more elaborate and had apparatus that reached into space, that attached to platforms serving as spaceports with links to space cities in operation before, during and after the last major Ice Age on Earth. Earth inhabitants have been spacefaring millions of years in the past and up to the present, that has nothing to do with the human overt or covert space programs by several Earth-based nations of modern times. Evidence has been removed and continues, under cover of wars, for much of the past ancient civilizations and Alien operations and their accompanying ancient space involvements.

Extraterrestrials such as the Serpents and Reptilians, are in fact less extraterrestrial than humans. Serpents and Reptilians spend more time on these lower planets than humans, keeping a low profile during the budding human space-age that is mere child's play considering what is truly happening in space continuously, behind the denial curtain created and sustained by local human leaders to further delude the masses. Alien realities remained covert and kept hidden by governments, religious institutions, mainstream media, the scientific community, and entertainment industry, for the purpose of their personal survival. Such industries fail when information contrary to the standardized propaganda reaches the critical mass and contradicts the new realities. Liberal use of denial and persistent attacks, ridicule and derogatory innuendos against the few that shun status-quo belief systems, are profoundly effective at slowing down and keeping down the awareness levels of humans on multitudes of Earth-like planets, throughout the galactic kingdom.

PROVING GROUNDS

Ages past, inside the underground Reptilian cities on Earth and other such planets, was a conglomeration of humanoids in various stages of designed developmental evolution. The manufacturing of humanoids of differing species, to be placed and scattered to locations around the planet, progressed rapidly through many stages. Reptilians captured beings from distant star systems, copulated with them and brought their resulting seed material to Earth and impregnated humanoids. Most of the beings used in any of the seeding projects were then returned to their homes afterward, having been abducted by "Aliens" and enticed to mate on the ships (UFOs). Captured was the DNA material and a small portion of the essence of soul-material belonging to the contributing beings. The resulting, quantifiable material was preserved and placed into storage on one of the hundreds of storage facilities orbiting stars in the galaxy and later retrieved.

Inside the massive networks of labyrinths deep under the pyramids and other structures, are proving grounds, where humanoids pitted against humans of various races that have sprung from the embryos of material captured by Reptilians from various places in the galaxy. The chambers are rapid learning centers, where simple instructions of basic survival skills get drummed into the mostly virgin humanoid minds. Hunting small animals, killing them and properly dressing the meat and then cooking it for immediate consumption and preserving portions for later use. Finding and using flint for making fire and tools, setting snares and assembling rudimentary tools from materials near their campsites and endless numbers of other strategies, obligatory to exist inside flesh and blood machinery (humanoid bodies).

Wild animals, native to where tribes of humanoids were located to live, were brought out of cages and set loose inside of mazes, for deadly encounters with humanoids for up and close encounters with the beasts. Humanoids and humans were placed into the same maze with hunting gear they made themselves (with a Serpent nudge). Ferocious animals got the better of the tribes and what remained of the humanoids and humans, moved to the next stage of learning; how to survive near-fatal wounds and damaged limbs, and how to avoid and protect themselves from horrendous animals existing in the area.

Humans and humanoids had to survive in areas where wild and deadly animals stalked them day and night. They had to learn or died by the beasts that existed only as a continuation of the learning curve placed on the human inhabitants of the raw new worlds coming online on repeated cycles in every galactic sector. Survivors had to adapt quickly while breeding and propagating and teaching their offspring what they had learned to stay alive in a barbaric land.

Tribes battled other human and humanoid clans that they, at some point, encountered inside of mazes, where survival of the fittest was a real and brutal life experience forced on them. Battles were contrived and planned in the spirit realm, where souls wagered against other souls before being placed into physical bodies and readied for battles (real battles). Bodies were pre-developed and constructed by Reptilians and souls suited up with the bodies that they would fight against man and beast, for cosmic honors and the bounty for the victors.

Inside of the pyramids, Serpents entertained and contained highly mysterious creatures from deep in the underworld. Such bizarre creatures radiated enormous amounts of power equivalent to nuclear fission, not of the atomic variety, but with surpassing powerful energy than came from atoms. The humanoid creatures stood more than ten feet tall (some shorter) with massive limbs. The supernatural beasts defied control even for the Serpents. The creatures had bizarre requirements, and their needs met in exchange for services rendered to the Serpents. Several of the beasts roamed inside of the pyramids and through the massive networks of labyrinths below the pyramids. The harvested cosmic beasts were transported to planet Earth inside colossal Alien craft from red hyper-massive stars within the Milky Way Galaxy by the Serpents.

Serpents blocked pertinent information about the creatures to all but themselves. Hundreds and sometimes thousands, of humans and predatory animals were placed into the underground labyrinth as sacrifices, when unfathomable radiant star creatures visited the pyramids. Perverse banquets arrayed with every kind of predatory animal, humans, humanoids, lions, bears, tigers, wolves, hyenas, crocodiles, leopards, cheetahs, wolverines, foxes, dogs, and many others exotic predators, became the prey to the radiant creatures.

I was not allowed to track through portions of the labyrinth due to parts being off-limits, except to the animals (humans too), cherry-picked to make the voyage for whatever reasons, and always unknown even to them, who mated and were toyed with by the devil beasts before being consumed (eaten).

Some paths from the labyrinth led into rooms, caverns, nooks and crannies that had no egress once entered, which sealed up permanently with whatever entered or fell inside. Primarily for humanoid and humans in the physical flesh and blood bodies that had physical contact with the bizarre star beings, that hadn't been eaten alive.

There were rooms that held spirit prisoners too, belonging to many kinds of beings that traveled to the pyramids from distant stars and captured like in a Venus fly trap. I attempted to avoid such rooms, sending Pi in before I entered the rooms to test for variation and type of containments. Pi passed for a spirit being and sometimes triggered the mechanism set into place by Serpents. I knew I couldn't pull anything over on the Serpents, and, gracefully in some instances, they allowed me leeway and flexibility when I did fall into their clever Serpent traps. Pi escaped the rooms, the few that closed in on Pi, where I might not have been able without a Serpent releasing me with a reprimand for placing my muzzle in forbidden territory. I had no guarantees that they would spare me had I fallen into any of the thousands of mysterious hidden traps in and around the pyramid compounds.

Rooms, caverns, niches or whatever cut into solid rock, granite, marble or any number of other types of stone, took up portions of the maze and its bewildering passages. Some rooms made from solid metals, gold, silver, copper, and blends of metals, alloys like bronze, electrum, nickel, aluminum, and numerous far more exotic blends unknown to humans, also filled up portions of the maze. Dissimilar materials like plaster, ceramics, porcelain, plastics, and various types of insulator materials, smooth and shiny with designs and prints like modern wallpaper, covered some of the walls inside the strange rooms.

One room I entered as a physical human to see what would happen to a human, began to spin every which way around me while I stood still inside of it, which created instant confusion in my mind that generated strange and bizarre images on the walls. The room stopped gyrating, and the images vanished the moment I converted back into spirit form. The room was not meant for spirit beings and had no effect on spirits. Images buried themselves into my physical mind (brain) and vanished with all the paraphernalia that was attached and that had embedded into my human brain. For me to have discovered what that cosmic virus contained and would direct me to do, at some future time, required that I remained in the physical form and waited for it to activate into whatever the program hid within it, demanded.

The process to unveil itself, the program embedded into human brains, generally required a lifetime to come to fruition, and only after several stages and episodes do such viruses appear and bloom. I had zero interest and little tolerance in living in the physical realm for any length of time, that limited my autonomy and my choice of surroundings to pursue further. The ability to jump through time loops could not trick the virus program into disclosing itself. Tampering with the virus caused the hidden program to self-destruct.

Portions of the maze was a psychological mind-trap and pain chamber for humanoid minds. Humans and humanoids who perished during their trials and in possession of a soul, the soul was captured and retained in special rooms, crypts, tombs from where the soul was processed further and then sent to various underworld strata or reincarnation chambers.

My endeavors spanned the physical and spirit realms on many levels of reality. Lost souls find themselves stuck between the physical realms and the spirit realms, a place like a purgatory and know not what to do to escape their quandaries. Their minds are a mass of confusion as they relive as in rerun episodes, in a loop of wayward lives and regrets. Swallowed whole by doubts and fear, the souls are frozen and can't move forward or backward. There are many such souls everywhere and plenty of spirit beings mostly helping, but some also hindering the progress.

Such souls can have one foot in the spirit realm (grave), and one foot in the physical realm; near death, but can't let go due to petrifying fear of what waits for them in the unavoidable afterlife. I stopped to help a woman plagued with medical maladies that looked like gorged ticks leeching on her soul, viewable only from the spirit side. I plucked the lesions of mostly imaginary maladies off her soul and watched as her flesh instantly healed itself. She survived and was a new woman and went back into her life with revived stamina. Some fixes are simple and only required a little push to get souls back in the game of the life they must live before they can move up, down or sideways.

There are many spirits that continually feed off the misery that is human ignorance; such beings torment and feast on the troubles they helped to implement and seed into the minds of everyday humans.

EROPMANOP STARS

Eropmanop stars resemble neurons inside brain matter that fire off information to various parts of the human body. Such stars in the web that connects and binds regions of space as a network of linked computers in the cloud. Eropmanop stars are guarded and protected by beings such as myself acting like soldier bees watching over a hive. There is no penetrating such stars by any types of beings, spirit or physical, which are not part of the Star from its inception (I originated from the star before my birth on Earth). Any unauthorized matter, being or craft instantly incinerates before reaching the star for those who fail to heed warnings repeatedly broadcasted from Eropmanop. Eropmanop stars exist inside the cluster of yellow stars and number in the hundreds of thousands per quadrant.

Eropmanop stars exist isolated from the cycles of birth and death subjected to all other stars. Eropmanop stars are outside the jurisdiction and influence of time and time-spheres and never change in structural compression. Information continuously flows to Eropmanop from its millions of members scattered throughout the quadrant and beyond and absorbed into its supernatural matrix. The enormous amount of incoming information changed nothing concerning the core structure of the star itself, which has the capacity of Black Holes to sort, shrink and store infinite amounts of information and material.

Eropmanop, a star of unmatched wonder and majestic beauty, is home to billions of souls spawned and given life for the purpose of gathering unique information from every niche and cranny inside the sector of galaxies of a small fraction of the universe. Most Eropmanop souls never return to the star of their birth, but continue forever to send and transmit back to the star, exotic materials and information, from wherever the cosmic winds take us. Even from beyond this universe, from other universes existing in numbers larger than the totality of stars in this one universe.

Eropmanop is mountainous, with uniformed spikes covering the whole surface of the star. Each massive spike rises thousands of meters above the planet and they have bases that are thousands of meters in circumference. The star is made of a highly dense material unknown to humans. It has the appearance of burnished metal, but is not a metallic compound. Each towering spike contains billions of grottoes and niches pockmarked into its surface, that give the towers the look of thousands of strange glowing eyes peering out into the darkness of space. Each domicile (eye) glows red in a backdrop of the darkness of space creating a magical and mysterious spectacle for the eyes and senses of those born of the star alone.

Eropmanop has no moons and no light source as do planets that revolved around stars. Eropmanop is the star and gives off no light other than the speckles of billions of red dots covering the external surface area, the skin of the whole star.

Much of what we of Eropmanop collect and store inside of the star, radiates out into the cosmic radio waves and blankets massive regions of space. Like osmosis, information suitable to any particular being makes its way to physical brain-tissue neurons, of the billions of spacefaring humanoids traversing space at any given time and place in the cosmic sector. Human brains pick up information non-stop, no matter where they are and store information on many levels of mind, conscious and subconscious minds, where information is retrieved daily and nightly, without cessation.

Humanoid minds need a constant flow of information into brain matter to keep the mind relevant and grounded to some level of reality. No less than the physical body and mind, require a constant flow of oxygen to keep the body and mind alive and active. Or the blood, to carry nutrients and oxygen to the brain and mind to remain alive and functional. And the consumption of food and water, to provide the nutrients for the creation and maintenance of blood. Remove any of those items and the physical returns to its basic state, spirit.

The spirit needs not the physical body, but the spirit exists on many levels of awareness both physical and spirit. The height of awareness is determined by the knowledge the spirit possesses or has access to. The physical brain is limited, of information it can retain and hold. Information leaks out of the brain constantly and, when not relished and replenished, it becomes irrelevant and useless. The subconscious mind is a gateway to the universal mind and connects the physical mind to the spirit realms where the universal mind resides. As long as the human brain functions properly, it receives a constant flow of cosmic information through the pipeline that is the subconscious mind (portal).

That subtle, cosmic information through the mind portal, mixed with information gathered from environments people find themselves in, provides a glimpse of who and what they are. Cosmic information filters into the conscious mind from the cosmic mind and saturates the brain during sleep-time via dreams and spirit beings. Most of the pertinent information humans rely on in their personal lives, comes directly from spirit souls as myself, who spill the beans into people's ears and minds, day and night, from the moment of their birth till the moment of their death, without ever a break.

I came from Eropmanop and mated with a female Serpent inside of a ship parked above planet Earth. The Serpent gave birth to a fetus that my soul would conform to during the first trimester inside of my human mother. My surrogate human mother was taken onto a ship and implanted with the fetus that I would inhabit during her third trimester, near its full development. Portions of my soul were inserted at several intervals before my human birth came to be and I entered the human hybrid body at that moment.

Before my birth on Earth, I existed inside of Eropmanop in one of the billions of compartments that held my soul essence in perpetuity (existed forever), before reactivating and coming to Earth. Over the span of existence, I frequently emerged from my cell on Eropmanop and migrated into the cosmos and entered the time spheres for explorations and propagation duties and other circumstances as an agent of Eropmanop. I continued my travels and adventures deep into new forms of societies and realities that merged or formed when dimensions converged and mutated to other dimensional forms of realities and existences in a perpetual cycle of unabridged consciousness and absolute awareness.

During my travels through time and space, I kept tabs on some humans in various places in their existence in any number of locations inside of time spheres. Diamonds in the rough, human souls who no longer needed to be in the rat race of the reincarnation cycle and were ripe fruit, primed to evolve to higher cosmic orders and places. As spirit beings from Eropmanop, we remain on the lookout for such humans, and at our exclusive discretion choose to bring or direct, prime souls into the spirit realm and make them candidates for Eropmanop.

I entered the dream world of such humans and took them on journeys to visit other cosmic realms, where they had been during past lives and explored deep-rooted desires with them. Seldom as a group and mostly individuals, who were allowed to meet with those people that had positive influences on their lives and some that followed them from one life to the next, or leapfrogging to bypass lives where their presence was not in need, or presented unwarranted challenges if they had entered.

Through prolonged encounters with those past associates, souls gradually matured and became eligible for drastic soul changes and, for some, was granted a choice to enter the fold of Eropmanop.

OLD SOULS

Souls never age, and therefore, no old souls or new souls exist, only souls. Souls, however, have categories, and many categories of souls exist in this universe and the many other universes, scattered in the infinite numbers of dimensions that boggle even the higher spirit minds. Human-type souls make up a large portion of the souls in this grand universe, that spin the wheels that turn the huge turbans, creating energy fields that sustain other types of soul-beings. Soul-beings that, in turn, slave non-stop, to bring havoc and knowledge to humans and their souls, which is part of a warped sense of symbiotic behavior for the grand prize of entering the spirit realm of enlightenment, for wearisome human souls.

At birth, a fully aware and conscious soul gets placed into a human mind inside of a human brain. The newly manufactured brain is a clean slate with little information about where it is and why it is. The fully aware soul is then stripped down to its base and, depending on why it was sent to exist in the physical world, may never realize, until death the answer.

Inside a slobbering, burping, pooping and crying baby, resides a soul with near infinite knowledge of the universe that birthed it in the first place during an ancient time in an infinite existence that, in reality, began only a moment ago. Such is a reality where time is an illusion. The vast portion of that knowledge has been placed on hold for the duration of that soul's life while in the physical realm.

Spirit beings create the illusions of time and the illusions of matter for the physical beings who go through the assembly process from birth to death, on a conveyor belt of time. Time is a tool used by higher spirits to facilitate a created reality from which humans exist. Each life is not by chance, but by deliberate creation by the higher beings who manifest every detail and every element that goes into the manufacture of one human life. Every moment that is lived and experienced by souls placed into the driver seat of each body, as it moves and travels through manufactured time on manufactured but invisible conveyor belts, is precise and calculated for each soul.

Soul-processing is ongoing, from the moment a soul is released to exist in the physical reality, for prescribed durations suitable for that soul type. Same as stars are born out of the heart of a galaxy's Black Hole and degenerate (decay) and die and return to the Black Hole at some point. A similar process of renewal, as in the four seasons, of spring, summer, fall, and winter, the cycle is never ending for the material matter in which human souls be cloaked inside, as a cocoon cloaks a caterpillar. Riding on the conveyor belt of endless reincarnation cycles, is fated to those mortals too stubborn to jump off. Most souls do escape, eventually, and move back to the spiritual world from where they originated.

Humans spend a huge part of their lives chasing things they have no idea why they chase, crave or desire. Searching for meaning in every detail of their lives, as if that is their sole purpose in life. Humans spend their whole existence inside of mazes crafted by Serpents and managed by Reptilians, filled with trapdoors, speed traps, and mysterious hidden rooms, disguised as jobs, careers, love affairs, marriage, children, hate, envy, and greed. Only to one day die, some from old age filled with regrets from the deceptive choices made. It's all manufactured to distil out the purity of the soul from the residue that accumulated systematically over previous embodiments. When that happens, the whole of the universe becomes available for exploration.

When I leave this universe momentarily, as I often do, I enter one of the endless new universes that exist like pages inside a massive book with infinite pages, where each page is a unique universe of unimaginable cosmic wonder, fluidity, and omniscient reality. I never cease to be awestruck, amazed, astounded, and surprised!

Like dipping a toe into the strange water, I have yet to immerse into other universes, fully. And now, I have entered into another universe in the library of existence perhaps never to return, entirely.

BOOKS BY THE AUTHOR

In League with a UFO Second Edition (177 pages) ...1997

Shrouded Chronicles (267 pages) 2000

A Day with an Extraterrestrial (159 pages) 2006

An Italian Family, Capisce? (197 pages) 2011

Israel Crucified (215 pages) 2012

Orphans of Aquarius (209 pages) 2012

UFOs in the Year of the Dragon (217 pages) 2012

Mars and the lost planet Man (215 pages) 2014

Graduation into the Cosmos (203Pages)..................2016

Planet Eropmanop (252 pages)..............................2017

BLOGS IN BOOK FORM

UFOs and Extraterrestrials are as real as the nose on your face Blog, 2005...(pages) Published in book form, 2011 (383 pages)

Coming clean on Extraterrestrials and the UFO Hidden Agenda...Blog, 2007-8

(357 pages) Part 1...2011

(329 pages) Part 2...2012

(303 pages) Part 3...2012

(329 pages) Part 4...2012

(291 pages) Part 5...2013

(351 pages) Part 6...2013

EXTRATERRESTRIAL SPEAK PART ONE (347 pages) 2015

EXTRATERRESTRIAL SPEAK BOOK TWO (277 pages)

2016

WEBSITES

ufolou.com

baldin.proboards.com

FACEBOOK. Lou Baldin

Made in United States
Troutdale, OR
08/09/2024

21903297R00157